CLOSING
FOR NETWORK MARKETING

Getting Prospects
Across The Finish Line

KEITH & TOM "BIG AL" SCHREITER

Closing For Network Marketing
©2017 by Keith & Tom "Big Al" Schreiter

All rights reserved, which includes the right to reproduce
this book or portions thereof in any form whatsoever.

Published by Fortune Network Publishing
PO Box 890084
Houston, TX 77289 USA

Telephone: +1 (281) 280-9800

Second Edition
ISBN-13: 978-1-948197-01-4
ISBN-10: 1-948197-01-4

CONTENTS

PREFACE

Sam Pitts has a wealth of quotes and jokes. He once told us,

> "We are not born to win or born to lose ... but we are born to choose."

Wow! This puts the decision where it belongs: on our prospects.

Our job as professionals? To help our prospects overcome their fear of change and uncertainty. Then, they can make a "yes" decision to move forward in their lives.

Yes, it is up to our prospects. We offer support so they have confidence in the results of their decisions.

If you read the prequel to this book, *Pre-Closing for Network Marketing*, then you already know that prospects make decisions quickly, before our presentations.

But, what happens after our presentations? What do we say? How do we conclude our transactions? How do we answer any nagging objections and move our prospects to enrolling now?

This book will give us the tools and techniques to finish our presentations successfully.

—Keith and Tom "Big Al" Schreiter

PREFACE

I travel the world 240+ days each year.
Let me know if you want me to stop in your
area and conduct a live Big Al training.

→ **BigAlSeminars.com** ←

FREE Big Al Training Audios

Magic Words for Prospecting

plus Free eBook and the Big Al Report!

→ **BigAlBooks.com/free** ←

IS THERE A MAGIC ONE-SENTENCE CLOSE?

My prospects said, "Sure, go ahead and explain how it works."

Things started well. As I explained the background of the company, I noticed a slightly glazed look in the husband's eyes. That didn't bother me. I cranked up my enthusiasm another notch.

As I explained the company's mission statement, the wife began giving herself a manicure. I sensed things were deteriorating. But it would get worse. And worse.

Ten minutes into my presentation, I looked at their faces. The husband's face began to twist. He looked like he had a parasitic worm painfully eating the inside of his brain. His wife wouldn't even make eye contact. No worries. Just 30 more minutes of mind-numbing data and I was sure they would change their minds.

Well, my presentation did not convince them. Here was my last hope. Yes, I would go for the "close."

Can you guess what happened?

They said, "No!"

But it was my best close. How could they refuse? I heard this close at a sales convention and the speaker said it worked for him.

And here was my first lesson in closing.

Closing doesn't happen one time at the end of the presentation.

Closing happens before the presentation. Then, their decision is re-considered in the middle of the presentation. And yes, our prospects must confirm their decision at the end of the presentation. Then, we can move forward.

Even though most prospects make their decisions early, we can still talk prospects out of joining with a boring presentation and an anti-social close.

I had just proved that.

So, what do we currently say to close our prospects?

Imagine this uncomfortable situation. We are sitting with our best prospects, a husband and wife, who seem to be interested in our business. As we finish our presentation ... dead silence. No one talks.

More dead silence. Someone has to break the ice and say something. Our prospects are content to sit and watch us sweat.

What are we going to say? We don't want to get rejected.

We must say something. Gathering our courage, we meekly say, "Do you want to join?"

"Please?"

"Our baby needs shoes!"

This is embarrassing.

If we don't learn what to say at the end of our presentations, this scene will repeat itself over and over during our career.

We don't want to say something stupid to our relatives or they will make fun of us at the next family reunion. We can't be pushy or else our co-workers will walk on the other side of the street when they see us.

Now is the time to learn exactly what to say, word-for-word. We must get our prospects to make decisions to move forward.

Some suggestions?

Closing is important. Why? Because if we don't close, we don't get paid. That should be a good enough reason.

If we don't have anything to say at closing, how will we handle objections? We hear:

- "I want to think it over."
- "I have to talk it over with my spouse."
- "I don't have any money."
- "I don't know anyone."
- "I am too busy."
- "It is not for me."
- "I am not a salesman."
- "I don't know how."
- "It is too expensive."
- "It is a pyramid."
- "Do I have to sell something?"
- "Is it one of **those** things?"
- "It is too good to be true."
- "So what is the catch?"
- "I can't talk to my friends."
- "I tried that once and it didn't work."

If we don't have a great close now, then when we will create one?

We don't want to be victims. We are proactive. That is why we learn better closing skills.

Experienced networkers know that closing isn't about an awesome final sentence. However, we do have to say **something** at the end of our presentations. Staring at our prospects is not a good plan.

A few years ago, we asked our newsletter subscribers to submit their best and worst closing sentences.

Would you like to know what others say at the end of their presentations? Here are some suggestions from the subscriber survey we did.

Subscriber-suggested final sentences.

- Which one would you prefer for your family?
- Is this the opportunity to freedom for you?
- If the economy gets better or worse in the future, wouldn't it be nice to know that it won't matter? Because you are now financially "set" for life.
- Well, that is it. The choice is yours. The freebie business or the fifty-dollar business? Which fits you best?
- I have answered all your concerns, so when will we start working together?
- Which part do you feel will benefit you the most?
- Does this sound like a good fit for you?

- Which plan fits your budget?
- Do you see an opportunity for yourself?
- What would you like to do as your next step?
- My advice is not to join, but you never listen to me [smile].
- That is all there is to it. The rest is up to you.
- So, which will be easier? Working until you are age 65 or older, or following a simple system to find 250 users of these products?
- Are you ready to get started now?
- Now I have answered all of your questions. You have told me how much you like what our team and company do. Are you ready to join and start the journey toward the freedom you spoke of so passionately?
- You said you would act if this met your criteria, and we have met your criteria. Would you like the _____ or the _____?
- Most people I show this to are impressed with the business model and join right away. What impressed you the most?
- Would it make sense that if we can do what I said we could do, that you would take the next step?
- So, is there any reason why you can't get started now and get yourself into training?
- I will personally work with you to build your business for the next 10 days. If you are not happy

with the results, I will personally call the office and get you a full refund.

- Does this sound like something that would interest you?

- Most people enjoy the presentation and respond favorably, but I am really interested in what you think.

- How can I help you make a good decision?

- This is a pretty good deal, isn't it!

We might look at these closing sentences and think, "Hmmm, some are good. Some have possibilities. Some would never work with my friends. Some are disgusting!"

That is normal. There isn't one special close that will work every time, with every person, in every situation. We all have preferences.

But, we can improve! We can and should create new and better closes.

We also asked our subscribers to submit some closing sentences they hated. Yes, they sent us high-pressure, anti-social, rude sales closes that are ugly.

Want to see what our subscribers submitted and have a laugh? Some are really, really bad. :)

Worst closing statements from subscribers.

Warning: Some of these are very rude and belong in trashy movies about sleazy salesmen.

- Do you want to pay with cash or a credit card?
- So, what is it going to take to put you into this business today?
- Any three-year-old can see it is a good opportunity. Do you have a problem with that?
- Which part of my presentation did you like best?
- On a scale of one to ten, how do you see your enthusiasm?
- Don't you love your family?
- Losers think … winners act!
- Now that I have shown you how to better your life, when are you starting?
- Even the wimpiest wifey or hen-pecked hubby can make a fifty-dollar decision without permission. So, are you in or not?
- What do you mean? After all the time we spent together, you are telling me that you have no interest in my opportunity?

- Do you know what your life will be like without this wonderful product?

- We have already discussed that, using different words. Care to be honest with me here?

- Would you like to get rich now or never?

- Why won't you join my business?

- Do you want it in red or blue?

- You know I love to collect autographs. Just sign here.

- So which part of the opportunity didn't you like? The part where you can save children's lives, or the part where you will make a lot of money?

- I want to bless you with this opportunity to keep food on your table.

- Which part of my presentation didn't you understand, so that I can repeat it to you more slowly?

- It only costs $2,500 to join.

- Do you want to be the only one on your block driving an outdated car? Of course not. Here is how we can change that.

- I can see you are salivating to get in this program.

- So, are you interested? No? Okay. How about now? How about now? Now? Now? NOW?

- Hmmm, I thought you would grab a good opportunity when you saw it.

- You want to go ahead and do this, don't you?

- What name do you want on your bonus checks?
- You would be great at this and you can make tons of money!
- You would be great at this and make **me** a ton of money!
- Do you want to join now or next Tuesday?

Are you disgusted with those bad closing sentences?

We need to improve not only our closing sentences, but also our entire timing and strategy on closing. After all, getting "yes" decisions is what we get paid for.

As professionals, we must move forward and learn a **variety** of closes. Not every close is appropriate in every situation.

We want to have an inventory of closing sentences that help our prospects overcome their fear and procrastination. Our products, services and opportunity can't help our prospects unless they say "yes" to our offer.

But let's have some fun first!

Before we do any boring explanations, we will look at some quick and easy closes. Ready for some basic closes we can use right away?

ASK AN EASY QUESTION.

When we close, we must get the other person to talk. If we do all the talking, nothing happens.

So how do we get other people to talk? By asking a question.

Here is the problem with asking a question. We hate rejection.

The solution? Instead of asking a direct "yes" or "no" question, we can ask a more subtle question to get a commitment. Then, if our prospects say "no" to our question, we still have an opportunity to continue the conversation.

I needed questions like these when I began my network marketing career. When I started network marketing, I was afraid to close. Well, it was worse than that. I didn't even know how to close. I had no clue what to say.

It wasn't my fault that I didn't know how to close. They didn't teach me how to close in school. But here is what happened when I joined network marketing. The company assumed I already had the skills necessary to talk to people correctly. Bad assumption. :)

When we start our business, our confidence levels may not be high. Plus, we will talk to our closest friends, so we want to be polite. But, we still have to close and get that "yes" decision.

Here is an easy, polite, rejection-free close to start with. Is it the best close? Of course not. But at least it is a close we can use comfortably, without risking everything. Here is what we could say:

"You seem to like what I showed you ... would you like to know how to get started?"

There. That wasn't so bad, was it?

No one should ever get mad or offended with that closing statement.

There are two possible answers to this question. Let's look at the options.

If our prospect gives us a "yes" answer, we can assume our prospect wants to join. We can start with the sign-up process. Pretty simple.

If our prospect gives us a "no" answer, it would sound something like this. "Not yet. I need to know more. Could you explain ..."

This means our prospect still has some comfort issues about moving ahead. No problem. We can assist.

What is the worst answer from a prospect?

What is the maximum rejection we can get from this question? Here it is.

We say, "You seem to like what I showed you ... would you like to know how to get started?"

Our prospect replies, "No. I don't want to go ahead with this. It is not for me. I appreciate your time, but I don't feel like moving forward on this."

Gee. That wasn't so bad. If this is the worst rejection we will ever get from this question, then our fears of closing should go away.

Sounds great, but are there more ways?

In our book, *The One-Minute Presentation*, we discussed three mini-close phrases. We can use these to put the decision directly on our prospects. Here they are:

- "Well, what do you think?"
- "The rest is up to you."
- "And that's it."

All three of these phrases require our prospects to respond.

No more pressure on us. The pressure is all on our prospects to reply with their decision.

Plus, these statements show our prospects we have confidence in our offering. Prospects love that. If they are going to come with us on our journey, they want us to be confident that we will arrive safely.

More phrases?

This is getting easier.

If we feel anxiety about closing our prospects, we could also use this closing statement.

It is polite. It puts the decision on our prospects. It is easy to say.

Here it is. Simply say to our prospects:

"So what would you like to do next?"

This question relieves our nervous prospects, and instantly turns off the "salesman alarm."

Again, our prospects have to talk. They must make a decision about what they want to do next. Our prospects feel they must continue the conversation.

If our prospects want to join, they will ask to initiate the enrollment process.

If there are issues remaining in our prospects' minds, now we get a chance to hear what these issues are. Prospects will tell us exactly what is holding them back. And that is okay. We can continue our conversation to help our prospects overcome these issues.

Our prospects feel that we have their best interests at heart when we use the phrase,

"So what would you like to do next?"

We are not speaking to them as if we have an agenda, or as if we are trying to earn money from them. Instead, they feel respected and know we are here to help them. We both feel good.

When we ask, "So what would you like to do next?"- our prospects tell us exactly what they want. We won't have to guess what our prospects are thinking.

What are some of the possible responses we can get to that question?

- "Please leave. I want to talk it over with my spouse in private."
- "Give me an application. I might as well start now."
- "Bring me a 30-day supply of the product to try. Then I can make my final decision."
- "Enroll me in the next training class. I want to start now."
- "Help me build my prospect list. I want a fast start."
- "Give me more information to read. I want more time to feel better about my decision."

"What would you like me to do next?"

Here is another version.

"What would you like to do next?" is a very low-key way to get a decision. But, there is another way that is even more subtle.

We can say to our prospects, "What would you like me to do next?" Now our prospects feel in control of the presentation. Stress levels go down. However, we are still asking for a decision from our prospects. They must choose the activity they want us to do. Here are some of their possible answers:

- "Show me how to get started."
- "Explain again how much I should order."

- "Pack up everything and go home. I need to think about this in silence."
- "Can you review with me again how much money I could make in my first 60 days?"
- "Is it possible that you could talk to my best friend also?"
- "Could you make my application effective on the first of the month?"
- "Could you come with me for my first presentations when I talk to my friends?"

The phrase, "What would you like me to do next?" makes our prospects feel in control, but their answer is actually a decision.

Ready for more phrases?

"What works best for you?"

The pressure is on our prospects to continue the conversation and make a choice. The phrase, "What works best for you?" is rejection-free for us. That is a good feeling. When we feel safe, it is easier to use these sentences and techniques.

What kind of an answer can we expect from the phrase, "What works best for you?" Here is an example.

"Well, I would like to start the business, but I want to limit my initial investment. I think my spouse would feel better if we were not risking a lot of money to get started. Of course, after we see a bit of progress, we would be 'all in' and do whatever it takes to make the business work for us."

When we give prospects permission to choose, we get to hear their real objections and concerns. Now they have permission to talk with us honestly. If we know our products and business would be the best choice for our prospects, we will want to hear their objections and fears. Then we can help them make a "yes" decision.

Putting the decision directly into our prospects' hands means no pressure on us. All the pressure is on our prospects. We can sit back and accept the decisions our prospects make. Network marketers are not the only people who do this.

Neil Taylor, from England, used to sell cars. Upon returning from the test drive, his prospect would ask, "Where should I park the car?"

Neil would casually say, "Well, if you want to buy the car, park here. If you don't want to buy the car, park over there."

Neil's prospect had to make up his mind!

"Would you like to do business with us?"

When we say this, our prospects know that the next step is up to them. It also allows prospects to tell us why they can't do business with us. For example, they could answer,

- "Yes, I would like to do business with you, but our finances are too tight right now."
- "I have to talk it over with my spouse first."
- "I am not sure I can do this business."

It is important to know why our prospects can't move ahead. This question will help us get that information.

The psychology of this question is that most people will want to say, "Yes." People like doing business with others. We are not asking them to buy, but only asking them if they would like to do business with us. This question is an agreeable way to get the closing process started.

"So what are you going to do if you don't join?"

Our prospects will describe the consequences of not joining. Yes, our prospects are now closing themselves. They remind themselves of the penalty for not taking action now.

A typical response might sound like this:

"If I don't join? I will have to ask my boss for a raise. That will be difficult. But if I don't get a raise, we won't be able to pay the minimum balances on our credit cards. That means no summer holiday for us or our children. So yes, we'd better get started with this business now."

Here is another way of asking this question. "So, do you think keeping your current plan, working at your job, is going to be the answer?"

Again, this gets our prospects to think and talk about their problems.

Prospects remember what they say, much more than they remember what we say to them. That is why we should listen as they tell us their problems.

If our prospects don't have a problem, then we don't have a solution. We become irritating salespeople pushing our agenda. But when our prospects know they have a problem, and can describe the consequences of their problem, they will want to fix their problem immediately.

Closing prospects is problem-solving, not solution-pushing.

Here are some examples of the terrible consequences of delaying a decision:

- Having to work longer at a boring job.
- Having to continue waking up to an alarm clock.
- Keeping children in daycare instead of having them at home.
- Having a limited income opportunity with the fixed-income job.
- Delaying the type of holiday the family wants.
- Hoping that the pension will be enough.

Thinking it over is expensive. Let's make sure our prospects can afford the luxury of keeping their lives the same.

"Doesn't it make sense ...?"

Analytical, green-personality prospects respond well to this question. Some examples:

- "Doesn't it make sense to take the money you are already spending and put it toward a healthier option?"
- "Doesn't it make sense that having an extra income makes it easier to pay off your student loans?"

- "Doesn't it make sense to save two hours of commuting every day by starting a business that you can work from your home?"

- "Doesn't it make sense to use the best skincare possible since our face is our best first impression?"

- "Doesn't it make sense to pay less for our utilities so that we can invest our savings elsewhere?"

- "Doesn't it make sense to start now so that you can begin the countdown to firing your boss?"

Yes, it does make sense to know exactly what to say when we close. We don't want to be searching for words at this critical moment.

The "How else?" close.

We can make it hard for our prospects to keep their problems. How? By forcing our prospects to come up with a better solution than the solution we offer. Simply ask questions such as these:

- "How else are you going to get that extra $300 you need every month to get caught up with your bills?"

- "How else do you think you can lose five pounds each month?"

- "How else do you think you can keep your skin from wrinkling more every evening?"

- "How else can you break the pattern of six-day work weeks?"

When prospects are not sure.

People hate making decisions. They want to procrastinate, which means they make a decision to stay where they are.

Point out the future consequences of not making a decision to move forward by saying:

"Yes, I understand that you have to make a choice ... to either move forward with this business, or not. Consider this. Five years from now you don't want to look back and think, 'Gee. I wonder what would have happened if I had taken that opportunity?'"

"If it could all be done tomorrow and it was free, what would you like us to do?"

This phrase put the decision back where it belongs ... with our prospect. We are empowering our prospect to tell us what we must do to close the sale.

This statement does put a bit of pressure on our prospect for closure. Now it is up to our prospect to call an end to the presentation by providing the information necessary to move ahead. This is much better than staring into space, hoping that someone is willing to talk first.

"Before you can make a decision, you need to know what it takes to build the business ..."

After making the above statement, the sponsor bridges into an explanation of the training program and the personal commitment needed to succeed. So even before our prospect spends a single penny, our prospect knows how much commitment is necessary. The statement also gives the sponsor one more chance to summarize the pertinent benefits from the presentation.

One definition of closing.

Closing does not have to mean high pressure or life-or-death consequences.

We could reframe the word "closing" in our minds to mean, "Helping support our prospects to overcome their fears and insecurities so they can move forward."

That should make us feel better.

GETTING PEOPLE READY FOR THE CLOSE.

How do we comfortably enter the closing part of our presentation? We don't want to abruptly announce our close by saying, "So that is the last benefit of our product. Do you want to buy?"

Obviously that's an exaggeration. But if we don't practice how we begin our close, we may sound nervous. That will cause our prospect to react with uncertainty.

Here are some words we can use to introduce our close to prospects.

- "Now, I would like to show you how I work with new distributors like you." (This also creates an assumption that our prospect will be joining us.)
- "Let me show you how most of our customers make their orders with us."
- "So if you would like to partner with me in this business, would it be okay if I showed you the next step?"
- "Would you like to know the next step?"

Sounds natural, doesn't it? We want to have a conversation, not a high-pressure interrogation.

Now, let's move on to a universal close that we will use over and over in our careers.

A CLOSE WE CAN USE ... EVERYWHERE.

We love this close. Why?

Because it fits almost every situation. Yes, it even handles the "I need to think it over" objection too.

This nine-word close is easy to remember. It is great for those situations where we feel nervous.

Our special close does this:

1. It stops the chit-chat, and asks our prospects for their decisions.

2. It gets the decision immediately with no rejection.

3. It shows our prospects that we want to serve them and that we have their best interests at heart. We want the decisions that help our prospects the most.

4. It relaxes our prospects by giving them clear choices.

5. Finally, it takes advantage of a subconscious mind program: that we choose what is easier, not what is harder.

All this with nine words?

Yes. Starting to love this close already?

Imagine that we finish our presentation. Dead silence. We will say:

"So, what is going to be easier for you?"

And then we give our prospect two choices. That's it!

This close tells our prospect:

1. Stop the chit-chat. It is decision time.

2. We want to know what our prospect feels is best for him.

3. We are not pushing our solution. We are giving our prospect choices.

4. We are asking our prospect to make a choice. Our prospect makes a choice. Done. No more thinking it over. No more procrastination.

5. And finally, what does our prospect want? Something hard or easy? Easy, of course.

"So what is going to be easier for you?"

The first choice is for our prospects to delay or make a decision not to move forward. They keep their current situation and their problems.

The second choice is our solution.

Simple, right?

For our prospects, there are two choices. They decide which choice is easier for them.

Choice #1: Continue life as it is.

Choice #2: Our solution.

Some examples.

"So what is going to be easier for you? To continue working that job you hate every day for the rest your life? Or, to get started with our business now, so maybe next year you can tell your boss good-bye?"

"So what is going to be easier for you? To continue getting by on one paycheck? Or to get started tonight, so you can pay for Christmas with cash instead of credit cards?"

"So what is going to be easier for you? To continue leaving your family at 7 AM every morning to go to a job you have no passion for? Or to start your part-time business tonight, so maybe next year you can be home with your children?"

"So what is going to be easier for you? To work hard every day for the rest of your life to help your boss build a big house for his retirement? Or to start working for yourself, so you can retire early instead?"

Could we use this for products and services too?

Certainly. Here are a few examples.

"So what is going to be easier for you? To allow your skin to get older every day? Or to stop the aging with our magic skincare cream?"

"So what is going to be easier for you? To continue paying the highest utility rates on your street? Or to fill out this simple four-minute application, to start getting the lower rates that you deserve?"

"So what is going to be easier for you? To continue locking the door every time those home-wrecking grandchildren come by to visit? Or to take our energy product ten minutes before they come, so the grandchildren will whine, 'Grandma, Grandma, slow down. I can't keep up!'"

Closing seems easier now, doesn't it?

Closing means moving our prospects forward to make a decision. As professionals, we want a variety of closes that we can use. This simple nine-word close will fit almost any situation we encounter.

So what is going to be easier for you? To continue feeling bad when it's time to close? Or to use these nine words to make closing easy?

Managing the Decision-Making Funnel.

Why do we limit the choices for our prospects when closing? There is an old saying that a confused mind always says "No" to our offers.

Complexity may work for us. This is the business that we love. But for prospects? They hate complexity. They want to make a simple choice, and then move on with their lives. They have too many decisions waiting in line, so they want to sort out the decision with us quickly.

We must make our choices simple. What happens if our closing statements are long and complicated? Our prospects will say "No" because they fear what they don't understand.

But what if our closing is too simple? Don't worry. Our prospects will ask us for more information if they need it.

Let's think about this simplicity from our prospect's viewpoint.

- At the end of our presentation, does our prospect understand the details of our compensation plan?

- At the end of our presentation, does our prospect remember all the background and credibility of our company?

- At the end of our presentation, does our prospect understand the science behind our product or service?

- At the end of our presentation, does our prospect know, word-for-word, exactly what to say to his friends?

Of course not. These are all "unanswered questions" in our prospects' minds. And what do we do?

We ask our prospects for the final decision. Ouch.

Of course our prospects will react by saying, "I need to think it over." And when our prospects think it over, they still don't have the answers to these questions.

Instead of torturing our prospects with this type of unprofessional presentation, we should manage the "decision-making funnel." We should direct our prospects' decisions to limited options.

For example, in the previous chapters, we limited the options to:

1. "Life as it is,"

or

2. "Join our business."

We should design our closing words to lead to limited choices.

This is kinder to our prospects, and we will succeed in getting a decision.

OFFER PROSPECTS THE CHANCE TO KEEP THEIR PROBLEMS.

This is an interesting close. It takes a bit more time, but our prospects appreciate the chance to see the big picture of their problems and our solution. When we use this close, we won't have to worry about buyer's remorse. This close eliminates the second-guessing that prospects sometimes have after making their final decision.

Step #1: De-stress our prospects.

We start our close by saying, "Let's make sure we are focusing on the real problem. If the problem is not that bad, sometimes it is easier to live with it for the rest of our lives. No need to change. No need to do anything about it."

How do our prospects feel now? De-stressed. Relaxed. This allows prospects to let go of any internal tension from our sales presentation. Now they can take a cold, hard look at their problems.

Our prospects can now focus their thoughts on the problems they want to fix. We know that if prospects don't believe they have a problem, then there is no need for a solution from us.

Step #2: Describe the problem.

Next, we describe our prospects' problems in our own words. This way the problems won't be vague. And, we can position the problems in the worst possible light if we need to. The purpose of the step? To reaffirm to the prospects that their problems exist.

For example, we might say something like this.

"We talked about your two-hour commute to work each morning, and the two-hour commute home each evening. Each day you lose four hours in stressful traffic away from your family. This will go on forever unless something changes."

We want to make sure our prospects' problems are at the forefront of their minds. We want them thinking about solving their problems, not about all the facts from our presentation.

Step #3: Decision time.

We continue. "How do you feel about keeping these problems? Or do you think this is something you definitely want to fix?"

The answer will be obvious from our prospects.

What if our prospects don't feel motivated to fix their problems? We can spend more time talking about the consequences and the pain of keeping their problems.

Summary.

Polite? Yes. This allows us to remind our prospects of their current pain with their problems. We can review the cost of keeping their problems. That cost could be in money, time, or quality of life.

This technique removes all those little side distractions that prospects have. This focuses their attention on the big picture: "Do I want to keep my problem, or do I want to fix my problem now?"

That's it. Our closing technique is to focus their thoughts on this one big question. "Do I want to keep my problem, or do I want to fix my problem now?"

When our prospects' problem is big enough, they won't question our solution. Their choice is to fix the big problem in their lives.

MAKE IT HARD FOR PROSPECTS TO KEEP THEIR PROBLEMS.

If our prospects do not accept our solution, then what are they going to do? They still have to fix their financial problems. So we ask them to come up with an alternative solution to our business opportunity. Usually alternative solutions are more difficult than starting a part-time business with us.

Here is a sample conversation.

Prospect: "I am not sure if I want to join your business."

Distributor: "As we discussed, you have a serious cash flow problem at the moment. You need an extra $500 every month. So if you don't join our business to earn that extra $500 a month, then what do you intend to do instead? The problem won't go away. You still have to get an extra $500 a month. Are you thinking of taking a part-time job every evening after you get home from work? What do you have in mind?"

Prospect: "I don't have enough energy or time to make a part-time job my solution. I don't want to work an extra part-time job for the rest of my life either. My 'winning the lottery' strategy hasn't worked well. I could borrow money from my

father-in-law, but that only makes the problem worse. So …
I don't know."

Distributor: "Well, if you and I can't think of any other
solution, this part-time business we talked about seems like
your best solution. Why not get started now, so we can get
that extra $500 a month to fix your problem?"

Prospects are human.

When prospects have a problem and don't have a solution,
they wish their problem would go away. But problems don't
just go away.

Our prospects prefer to change the subject, or turn their
thoughts to something else. They don't want to face the pain
of their problems.

Our job is to help our prospects move forward and fix
their problems. That is why we must hold our prospects'
attention. Prospects need to realize that we have the best
available option.

One more idea on this …

A simple closing question.

Try asking this question with difficult prospects:

"How long can you wait?"

Some prospects say that they don't have time to build a
business, but want to add $500 a month to the family budget.
In that case, we will ask them how long they can wait until
they start earning that extra money.

Our prospects might say that they need more income now. Or, maybe they will say that they can only wait six months or a year. Regardless, they are admitting they will eventually need more money.

This question assumes that our prospects will join, and that their only decision is how soon to join.

It makes our prospects think of the consequences of not joining and never having that increased income.

A WORD OF CAUTION.

Powerful closing skills make it easy to summarize our benefits and get prospects to take action. However, there are two types of decisions:

1. A decision of commitment, and

2. A decision of convenience.

Uh-oh. Yes, we must respect each prospect's situation. We will use our skills to get our message past all our prospects' filters and alarms. Now, once our message is inside our prospects' brains, we should let them decide what is best for them.

If we push our agenda and needs above our prospects' needs, they might make a "decision of convenience." That means it was easier for them to say "yes" than it was to say "no."

A decision of convenience is weak. It means the first obstacle may crush their businesses. Even a small amount of rejection and criticism would be too much for them. We would constantly have to reinforce their decision of convenience. That might be more work than we have time for.

We want our prospects to make decisions of commitment. We can accomplish this with our professional closing skills. We won't need artificial or overpowering closing statements to get this commitment. Why? Because our prospects should already be sold before we finish our presentation.

So it is okay to have prospects tell us "no" during our presentation?

Of course. We should have their best interests at heart. If we believe in our products and opportunity, we should want them for our prospects.

If our products and opportunity are not a good fit for our prospects, that is okay. We want to help our prospects make the best and most beneficial decisions they can.

But what about those uncertain situations where we can benefit our prospects, but their fears hold them back? For example, during our presentation we ask, "Do you feel this product would help?"

Our prospects answer, "No."

That is good feedback. If our prospects don't feel that the product has enough value, now would be a great time to know. We could then discuss additional benefits that might be more appropriate for our prospects.

Prospects can sense our intentions.

We shouldn't be afraid of negative feedback, objections, or questions if our motives are to help our prospects. We want our prospects to feel that we have their best interests at heart. Then they will be more open about their feelings, fears, and doubts.

Our presentation won't be a win-lose contest. Instead, our presentation will be filling in vital information that our prospects want. This makes it easier for them to move forward with their initial enthusiastic "yes" decision.

Remember, our prospects have already made one positive "yes" decision, or else they wouldn't be meeting with us.

TWO BASIC MOTIVATIONS.

As humans, our internal wiring is simple. Two of our basic motivations are:

1. To seek pleasure.

2. To avoid pain.

This is not hard to understand. For example:

- If a person is unable to lose weight, the pleasure of overeating is greater than the pain of being overweight.

- If a person is procrastinating, there is greater pleasure in maintaining the status quo, than stepping out of his or her comfort zone and taking action.

Which motivation should we choose to help our prospects make a decision?

Pain. Pain works the best. Yes, we will do much more to avoid pain than we will do to seek a reward. So if we are closing our prospects, what should we concentrate our conversation on?

Pain.

Amateur network marketers summarize all the pleasure points of their great presentation. They talk about their breakthrough technology, the testimonials, the beautiful new life in the future. This is nice. But this is weak motivation to most prospects.

What happens when we talk about pain? Prospects make quick decisions to avoid pain. So, we need to talk about our prospects' problems, help them focus on their problems, and ask them to tell us the consequences of not fixing their problems.

This is how professionals get prospects to make decisions.

Closing statements.

To show the difference between focusing on pain instead of pleasure, here are two closing statements. See which one you think would be more powerful.

Pleasure.

"Mr. and Mrs. Prospect, there has never been a better time to join our business. We are gaining momentum and are at the forefront of our industry. As pioneers in our field, we have received awards from many of the major media channels. They agree with us that our business is the future.

"Now is the best time to join because we just installed our new compensation plan, version 4.0. This allows us to earn even more on our bonus points that we did before.

"With hundreds of testimonials, and our management's 206 years of combined business experience, we are primed for success.

"Mr. and Mrs. Prospect, do you want to start now?"

Pain.

"Mr. and Mrs. Prospect, as we discussed, life is not forever. If we continue spending our waking hours commuting and working away from our children, that time will never come back. We want to be with our children during their formative years. This is our chance to make a difference in our children's lives.

"I know that working two jobs feels like we are warehousing our children in daycare. This is our chance to create enough part-time income to quit those second jobs. Then, we can spend that precious time with the children. It won't take much from our business to replace those part-time jobs. So, Mr. and Mrs. Prospect, do you want to start now?"

What do you think?

Feel the difference?

When we talk about benefits and pleasure, it seems to go to the logical part of our minds. When we talk about pain, the response is much more emotional.

Decisions are emotional activities. Case studies show that to get prospects to decide to move forward, emotion is a requirement. Pain creates emotion effortlessly.

Now, what will you focus on in future closing statements? Pain, of course.

It's easier on both our prospects and ourselves when a decision is made quickly.

WHEN THE PAIN IS BIG ENOUGH, OUR PROSPECTS WILL CLOSE THEMSELVES.

Zig Ziglar tells the story of an old hound dog. The hound dog moaned and whined as he laid on a nail on the front porch. So why didn't the dog get up off the nail? Because for the dog, it was easier to lay on the nail and complain than to get up and move.

This also describes our prospects. Prospects don't like change. They will put up with low levels of pain rather than take action to stop the pain. Only when the pain is big enough will prospects take action to fix their pain. Here is an example.

Coffee break.

Several co-workers crowd around the coffee machine. The first worker complains, "I hate commuting to work. The traffic is so bad."

We say, "Would you like to join me in checking out an opportunity to work out of our own homes?"

The first coworker replies, "No! I don't have time to check out an opportunity. When I go home, I only have enough energy to watch television."

The second coworker complains, "This job doesn't pay enough. I need more money for my family. Everything is so expensive now."

We say, "Would you be interested in a part-time bonus check?"

The second coworker replies, "No! Those things never work for me. I don't want to even try. I don't care what it is. I don't even want to hear about it. Now, let's get back to complaining about the recent price increases."

The third coworker complains, "I am so bored at this job. It has no meaning. I want to have a career that is more fulfilling."

We say, "Would you like to look at my business? We help lots of people. Plus, we get to take five coffee breaks a day."

The third coworker replies, "No way! I don't know anything about business and I don't want to learn. I tried learning in high school and it didn't work out. I am not trying that learning thing again."

Our co-workers are like the old hound dog on the nail. Complain, complain, complain. But their current pain is not big enough to motivate them to get off the nail. They decide to live in low levels of pain for their entire life, and never take a chance to get up off that nail.

The dentist.

Are dentists great closers? Do they have great selling skills? No. But dentists don't have to be salespeople. Why? Because they know a secret.

What is the secret to the selling success of dentists? They know that, "When the pain is big enough, people will close themselves."

Dentists don't need sales techniques. All they need is the ability to solve the prospects' problems. Here is an example.

Imagine we get a toothache. It hurts. It is annoying. And now it is steadily getting worse. We can feel the throbbing inside of our head. The side of our face is starting to swell. We can only see out of one eye. We can't chew our food and we have to suck our meals through a straw. The ringing in our ears is deafening. The pain is unbearable. Even the strongest painkillers don't work. We call our dentist.

When we call our dentist, he says, "I'm sorry. We are booked up for the next three weeks. I can set an appointment for you three weeks from now."

What do we say? Do we say, "Oh, that sounds okay. I will wait three weeks for my appointment."

No! We don't say that!

We are in pain. We've made an instant decision to fix that problem now. We say to the dentist, "I am coming into your office now. I will sit on the sofa in the waiting room and wait for someone to cancel. I will take their appointment. If no one cancels their appointment in the morning, then during lunch, while you are eating your sandwich, look inside my mouth!"

Well, no one cancels their appointment in the morning. During lunch, our dentist is eating his sandwich. He looks inside of our mouth and says, "Oh, that looks bad. That tooth is going to have to come out. It will cost $400 to have that tooth removed."

What do we say? Do we say, "Would you take $395?" No! We don't say that! We don't negotiate for a lower price. We say, "Take that tooth out now!"

The toothache pain is so bad that we don't need a sales pitch. We don't need to look at x-rays. We don't need a brochure. We don't need a finance plan. We want that tooth out now and we want the pain to stop.

When the pain is bad enough, we close ourselves.

What is the lesson here?

The lesson is that people have problems. People will keep their problems until the pain is too great. Then they make a decision to fix their problems.

What does this mean for us? This means that we should not offer solutions to our prospects until they want to fix their problems.

No solution until they want to fix their problems? Yes.

Our job is to magnify their pain to such unbearable levels that they want to fix their problems now. Yes, our job is to make our prospects' lives more miserable by focusing them on their problems.

How do we do that?

In our book, *Pre-Closing*, we used four little words to get prospects to focus on their painful problems. You might be wondering what those four little words are.

Are you okay with never knowing what those four words are?

Are you okay with never knowing how to get prospects to make immediate decisions?

Are you okay with never knowing these four magic words while other networkers do?

Are you okay with wasting time with prospects who are not ready to make a decision?

Are you okay with begging people to move forward while they insist on staying indecisive?

Are you okay with seeing these words over and over again until you notice the pattern?

It is obvious, isn't it?

Prospects feel their pain when we use the words, "Are you okay with ...?"

If we intensify their awareness of that pain, prospects will make an immediate decision to move forward.

We can use these four words not only at the beginning of the sales encounter, but also at the end of the presentation. But for now, let's focus on a few examples of using these words at the end of our presentations.

Ready?

- And that is how our business works. So, let me ask you this. Would you like to get started tonight with my help, or are you okay with continuing your current working schedule of six-day work weeks?

- And that is our complete program. Let me ask you what works best for you. Are you okay with continuing to try to get by on one paycheck, or should we start your part-time business now, so you have that extra money you want for Christmas and family vacations?
- Well, that's everything. The company, the products, and how we get paid. So, would you like to start the countdown to firing your boss tonight? Or are you okay with staying in your current situation?

And yes, we can do something similar for our products and services too. We encourage you to take some time to create examples for your business.

With just four words, we can get prospects to focus on their problems and make an immediate decision to fix them.

One way of looking at this is that our job is to "induce more pain." The bigger the pain, the faster the decision.

Closing prospects is easy when they do the closing themselves.

THE TWO-ENVELOPE CLOSE.

We create two sealed envelopes for our opportunity meetings. Label one envelope "No" and the other envelope "Yes."

At the end of the meeting, we show our guest the two envelopes. We say, "You will get one of the envelopes depending on your decision."

If our guest says "No" to our opportunity, we give our guest the "No" envelope that contains discount coupons for our products or services.

If our guest says "Yes" to our opportunity, we give our guest the "Yes" envelope that contains discounts and offers for training, extra fast-start packs, prospecting tools, etc.

Our prospect is now forced to make a decision. Our prospect has to tell us which envelope he wants.

Now even the shyest new distributors can ask for a decision from their guests. All the new distributors have to do is say:

"Hope you enjoyed the explanation of our opportunity. I have two envelopes here. One of them is for you. If you would like to join, take the envelope that says 'Yes.' And if this opportunity is not for you, simply take the envelope that says 'No.'"

HERE IS YOUR ONE-DOLLAR BILL.

This is an easy close that only costs us one dollar. We can use this close at the end of an opportunity meeting, or if we sit down with a single prospect, or a couple.

We give our prospects the $1 bill and say these words:

Take a good look at this one-dollar bill. This one-dollar bill now belongs to you. You can do three different things with this one-dollar bill. What you choose to do is up to you.

#1. You can spend it. You can go buy a can of soda or a small candy bar.

#2. You can frame it. Yes, you can buy an inexpensive frame, put this dollar bill inside the frame, and put it on your wall. It will be there for you to admire it. And on the plus side, you would be one dollar ahead in your financial future.

#3. Or finally, you could use this one-dollar bill towards the cost of starting your business tonight.

Do whatever you think will help you the most!

But please, don't have any regrets. One year from now, I don't want you to take a look at your framed one-dollar bill and say, "I wish I would have joined that business. I could be earning an extra $500 a month now. Instead, I have this nicely framed one-dollar bill."

What happens next?

The prospects must make a decision. They are holding that one-dollar bill. Now our prospects must decide what to do with that one-dollar bill.

ALL IS NOT LOST.

Some prospects will turn down the opportunity to join us in our business. That's okay. Today may not be the right time for them. However, they will forget about our opportunity, unless we remind them.

Here is what we can do to keep our business fresh in our prospects' minds.

Imagine that a friend from work turns us down. He says,

"Oh, I don't know. I am not sure this business will work for me. I don't want to spend $200 to get started in this business."

Go to a store and buy an inexpensive picture frame. It might cost about $3 or less.

Now, ask our friend to write out a $200 check - and then void it. Place the $200 check in the picture frame and ask our friend to hang the frame in his home, somewhere where he can see it.

Tell our friend:

"By not joining our business, you will save that $200. You can now invest that $200 in something else. Maybe you will get lucky and hit a hot stock or even win the lottery. Let's see how well that $200 works for you over the next three months or six months. I will check back with you in a few months."

That $200 might have opened the door to hundreds of extra dollars a month in our prospect's new business. However, our prospect made the decision to turn down our opportunity ... for now.

Every time your prospect looks at that picture frame, he will think of us and our opportunity.

And that is what we want.

When the time is right for our prospect, we want our prospect to be thinking of us.

Plus, we have an excuse to follow up in three months or six months. And what are the odds that our prospect will win the lottery or pick a hot stock during that time? Very low. We will have an open-minded prospect for follow-up, who just lost three months of his life to indecision.

And all this on a tiny $3 investment.

Or we could position the $200 in this way.

We could say to our prospect, "You can decide not to start our business today. Instead, you can keep your $200 in your savings account. After one year, you should have an extra dollar or two in interest. How you choose to invest that one or two dollars is up to you."

What is our prospect thinking? "One or two dollars in interest won't even pay for a cup of coffee. I need a different solution for my life."

And now we have another opportunity to help our prospect make a decision to join.

SOFTER WORDS.

Harsh, direct words create tension. That is the last thing we want when we are helping our prospects make their final decisions.

By carefully selecting our words, we can guide our prospects to open up and tell us their real concerns.

Isn't that what we want?

Here are some examples of taking our old version of harsh, direct words, and revising them to sound more prospect-friendly.

Old words: "What exactly is causing you to hesitate?"

New version: "I am just curious. What possible problems do you see in your way?"

Old words: "What do you mean that it costs too much money?"

New version: "Yes, we are paying more for a reason. Let me review that with you quickly."

Old words: "What exactly is keeping you from making a decision tonight?"

New version: "Is there any reason that you might feel this would be an unwise decision?"

Old words: "Why do you need to think about it?"

New version: "Yes, we need to think about these decisions. Here are some benefits we should consider."

Old words: "This is why that shouldn't bother you."

New version: "Would you like me to tell you about others who had that same concern?"

Old words: "Why don't you want to be a salesman?"

New version: "Of course we don't want to be salesmen. Instead, we want to be connectors, helping others get what they want."

Old words: "Want to sign up and become a distributor?"

New version: "Would it be okay if we went into business together?"

Old words: "So would you like to start now and make sales presentations all day?"

New version: "Would it be okay if you had a fun business talking with prospects while taking five coffee breaks a day?"

Small changes in our words make a huge difference. One of the most important skills in network marketing is learning proven phrases that help our prospects hear our message clearly.

These are examples of how changing what we say can make our prospects feel more comfortable with their decisions.

Remember, our prospects are under a lot of pressure to make sure they make the right decisions. They don't want to appear foolish or make mistakes.

We don't want to add to their internal pressure and create more tension by choosing the wrong words.

The million-dollar close.

What is the million-dollar close?

It's a simple, rejection-free way to get our prospects to make a decision.

- No hype.

- No pressure.

- No tricky sales manipulation.

- No neurolinguistic spin.

- No hypnotic mind-control.

Just a simple close between two people.

If we hate the phony sales manipulation closes, we will love this straightforward approach to building our business.

Let's first look at how salesmen learned to close prospects in the past.

First, there was the "Ben Franklin Close" to help the prospects see things from the salesman's viewpoint. Here is an exaggerated example of this:

Prospect: "I can't decide."

Salesman: "Well, when old Ben Franklin had to make a decision, he used to weigh the pros and cons and go with the option that seemed best. Why don't we do that?"

At this point the salesman got his prospect to agree. Then the salesman listed 8,000 reasons why his business is awesome and said:

"Well Mr. Prospect, that's 8,000 reasons you should join my business. Can you think of 8,001 reasons why you shouldn't?"

Of course the prospects couldn't think of that many excuses on short notice, so the prospects felt threatened and inferior.

Then there is the "Pin Down" close. It goes something like this:

Prospect: "So I could make some extra money doing this?"

Salesman: "If you could make some extra money and I could show you how, would you be willing to sign right now?"

Prospect: "Ugh, where is the shark repellant?"

Prospects hate it when salesmen use their words against them.

And then there is the "Math Close."

The salesman calculates the cost of the program and reduces it to a daily or hourly number.

For instance, if it cost the prospects $100 per month, the salesman would represent that as only $3.33 a day ... or only 14 cents per hour!

Salesman: "You can see why this is such a great program."

Prospect: "No, I really can't."

Salesman: "Well, look at it this way. Are you willing to invest just $3.33 a day if I could show you how to turn that into $273.97 per day?"

The prospect thinks, "I can't multiply that in my head that fast. I will just play along until I figure a way to get out of this sales presentation."

How do we feel about using these old-school closing strategies?

Do we feel comfortable backing people into a corner and forcing them to make a decision?

Do we feel like a salesman instead of a partner?

Do we feel that we come across as a salesman instead of someone who is trying to help?

Most people are uncomfortable using these win-lose closing strategies.

Here is another issue to consider.

These closing techniques are the same ones used to sell cars, washers, appliances, insurance policies, etc. These may be one-time transactions.

But our network marketing opportunity is not a one-time sales transaction. We are looking to build relationships with our new partners for the life of our business.

It is one thing to "sell" a product, take the money, and never see the prospect again. But is that what goes on in network marketing?

No. In network marketing, we are going to see that person again and again. By using these high-pressure closing techniques, it puts us into the position of saying:

"We shamed and tricked you into signing up, but from now on, we are going to treat you like an adult."

These sales closing techniques may sell an insurance policy or some other one-time-sale product. However, they may not be the best way to build relationships with our future leaders.

We could easily name many more old-school closing techniques, but let's move on to the "million-dollar close."

Why is the "million-dollar close" better?

Selling and high-pressure closing feels adversarial. Most networkers would rather be a partner, a consultant, a coach, or a teacher. Networkers like helping someone succeed.

Networkers want to motivate and lead their undecided prospects into decisions to move forward. Unfortunately, most prospects find it easier to never make a decision.

So what do we do as networkers?

We cajole, plead, bargain, manipulate, and force prospects to commit. We become the high-pressure salesmen we despise. And, we don't enjoy the process of closing.

New network marketers who haven't learned any skills are terrible in this role. Fortunately, prospects are saved from a constant bombardment of awful presentations and closing methods because these new network marketers never quite adapt.

Sadly, some network marketers continue on to become great high-pressure closers. They leave a trail of people persuaded against their will to join their program. Then they wonder why they have so much inactivity and "dead wood" in their organization.

They also wonder why no one can duplicate their success.

High-pressure closers eventually lose all respect for their prospects. They discard and ridicule people they consider to be "losers."

So, who are the best networkers?

Look at the top networkers. Many of them are mothers, teachers, or social workers, or in other similar, nurturing professions. Only a small percentage of top networkers are sharks or high-pressure salesmen.

Why?

Because we can't high-pressure prospects into becoming volunteer workers. People in network marketing are volunteers. They must want to work the business.

If we use high-pressure closes on our prospects, they will say "Yes" to get rid of us. Then they disappear.

If we allow our prospects to volunteer to join our business, then we have a more productive organization. That is why the mothers, teachers, and social workers do so well. They allow people to volunteer to join.

All of them use some version of the million-dollar close.

The million-dollar close allows prospects to:

1. Qualify themselves as a volunteer.

2. Join because they want to join.

3. Feel that they are making the decision based upon their choices, not ours.

The million-dollar close allows us to treat our prospects as adults, who can decide what they want in their lives.

You already saw the million-dollar close earlier in this book.

Yes, you read it, but it was so normal and low-key that it was "under the radar." Most people never even notice it. Now that is good news. This means our prospects won't feel alarmed when they hear it.

So what is the million-dollar close?

It is very simple. Present our network marketing opportunity in the most hype-free, honest way we can. Make sure we answer the basic questions our prospects want to know.

This completes our duty to our prospects. They receive the information they need to make an intelligent decision.

We finish our presentation by saying:

"Well, what do you think?"

That's it. That is the million-dollar close.

The rest is up to our prospects.

Our job is to sit back and listen. We delivered the information. We are not responsible for the decisions our prospects make in their lives.

And what happens?

Our prospects may tell us what they really think!

We will hear things such as:

"Looks interesting. So how do I join?"

"Is this one of those pyramid schemes? I don't think I would feel comfortable presenting this to my friends."

"You say that it is only $49 to sign up? That's very reasonable, especially with the money-back guarantee."

"Do you really think I could do this with your help? How much help could you give me?"

"I am busy now. My daughter is getting married next month. Let's visit after the wedding."

"It sure would be good if I could earn enough to quit my job. I hate commuting every day and putting the children in daycare."

"That sounds too hard. It's not for me."

All this feedback from one simple question.

When we use the million-dollar close, magic happens. Our prospects feel like we respect their feelings. And now, our prospects can openly tell us what they think.

We will notice that our prospects will fall into these categories:

1. Volunteers. These prospects think we have a great opportunity and are ready to join. These prospects join without the griping, complaining, and foot-dragging that sap our energy.

2. The prospects who say "No." This is okay. They feel good that we respect their decision. We feel good that we don't have to drag them with us on our journey to success. Not everyone has to be a member of our organization, right?

3. The prospects who have interest, but also have questions. These prospects feel that they can ask us questions without our high-pressuring and manipulating every question into a close. We will enjoy open conversations with these prospects.

Isn't this what most of us want out of our business?

Now we can relax, give pleasant, hype-free presentations, and allow our prospects to make their own decisions. When we treat our prospects as adults, they appreciate our behavior, and reward us accordingly.

Is this close too soft?

Some people might say, "Oh, don't ask what your prospects think. That will give them a chance to turn us down or bring up an objection. You need to force them into a corner!"

Hmmm. Aren't we here to help our prospects? If our prospects have concerns or doubts, we want to know about them. Then, we can give our prospects the confidence to move forward in spite of these doubts. All prospects have doubts. We might as well find out what they are.

The "qualify first" close.

Here is how to get our prospect to start building his business before he even joins our business.

We tell our prospect that he must "qualify" to join our program.

We could say this:

"Mr. Prospect. I don't want you to join my business if it is not for you. So, before you make a decision, do this. Come to next week's opportunity meeting and bring two guests. After the meeting, see how your guests react. See how you feel about our business. And then, make a decision."

Here is what happens.

1. Our prospect feels relaxed. He doesn't have to make a decision right away.

2. Our prospect will find it easy to bring two guests. There is no pressure on the guests. They are just coming to look.

3. Our prospect doesn't feel that he is trying to make money off his guests. He doesn't pressure them or himself during the invitation.

4. Now we have three prospects at the opportunity meeting instead of one prospect.

5. If our opportunity meeting is good, our prospect is off to a great start. He will have two potential distributors ready to go. And, more importantly, our prospect knows that he can invite guests and build a business. He just did it!

Or ...

We could also phrase this "qualify first" close in another way.

First, we give a complete presentation to our prospect. When our prospect says that he wants to join, we could say this:

"The only way that you can join us is to set appointments for your first two presentations. If you can't set these two appointments, well, I don't think this business is for you."

What will our prospect do?

Our prospect will immediately get on the telephone and set appointments for two presentations.

HUMANS LOVE EXCLUSIVE OFFERS.

Think about first impressions. If we can make our offer seem more exclusive, our prospects will want it more.

First, let's look at how **not** to do it. We don't want to start off by saying, "I am looking for five new people to work with."

What would our prospects think? "Oh, you are looking for anybody that breathes. Here comes the sales pitch." This is not a good way to start or end our presentation.

But what if we said this?

- "Our business works best for families that have a secure career or job. They use the extra money from our business to pay off debt, invest more, and retire early. Does that fit you?"

We didn't have to be a mind-reader. We learned their situation earlier in the conversation before our presentation began. By adjusting our words to make it more exclusive, the family feels good about our presentation.

Let's try another one.

- "If you are happy with your job and the hours you have, our business is not for you. Our business is for people who want a brand-new career."

What type of prospects would we say this to? To people who hate their jobs and want more in life. This opening helps our prospects think, "Yes! This is the business for me. Please show me how this works." The prospects feel like we are talking directly to them.

Imagine we are talking to a university student. What do we know about this university student? He will be unemployed when he graduates. His first job won't pay well because he has no experience. He will be starting his life with huge school loan payments. What could our "exclusive" summary be to him?

- "University students benefit the most from our business. Why? First, they can build it in their spare time while they are still at university. Second, with only modest success, their business can completely pay off their student loans. But third, for some university students, they can be their own bosses and have a full-time career immediately when graduating from university. They won't have to interview and hope for some low-paying starting position."

Now, what would the university student think? "This sounds perfect for me. If I can get a successful business early in my life, then I can travel and do the things I want. And I won't have those huge university debt payments hanging over my head."

Could we use this exclusive closing for our products or services?

Certainly. Let's do a few quick examples that help our prospects feel exclusive. This helps them make "yes" decisions easily. We get to highlight our unique advantages and separate ourselves from the competition.

- "Because our new diet program is formulated for people over age 40, this will give you the best chance to reach the weight-loss goals you desire."

Well, if we were over age 40, what would we think? "So that is why all my other diets failed. They were generic diets designed for everyone. What I need is a special formulation for people over 40. Here is my chance to actually lose weight."

- "What I just showed you was our premium utility plan. This is for people with A+ credit who own their own homes. Their credit worthiness helps them save money."

What would homeowners with good credit think? "This is for me."

- "Our toothpaste is for people who appreciate natural, safe ingredients. Anyone can buy a cheap toothpaste with chemicals, but we don't want to put chemicals in our mouths twice a day."

Here is what a mother with small children is thinking. "I want all-natural, safe toothpaste for my children. I don't want to stuff chemicals in my children's mouths twice a day."

"Yes" decisions come from happy prospects.

Prospects like to feel special. They like to feel that they are part of an exclusive group.

The more targeted our message, the easier it is for our happy prospects to say "yes" to our presentation.

Closing to groups.

When closing our presentations to a group of people, sometimes we feel uncomfortable.

Mark Davis is the author of *How To End our Speech with Confidence: 5 Closing Methods to Finish Like A Pro.* Let's take a quick look at some phrases he uses that gives our audience permission to make their decision ... now.

1. "When I finish this business presentation in two minutes' time, you can leave right away ... or you can walk to the back of the room for a snack and a drink. By the way, our cookies are delicious."

2. "When I finish, here is what you can do next. Talk to the person who invited you here this evening for details on how you can start. Or, if you have more questions, come to the front of the room and talk to me. I will gladly answer any questions."

3. "When I finish here, you can start your business by filling in the application. Just start at the top and write your name."

4. "When I finish talking in about two minutes, you can decide to continue living as you have in the past. Or, you could visit with me before you leave, and talk to me about the changes you are ready to make."

5. "When my talk finishes in ten minutes, you can ask me a question, fill in the order form, or log on and subscribe to the email updates."

6. "When you leave today, you can start writing a list of prospective customers for this product. Who do you know that wants to look younger and have more energy?"

If you do a lot of group presentations, I highly recommend reading his book.

REMOVING THE UNSPOKEN OBSTACLE.

The ad read:

"For Sale: Parachute. Only used once, never opened, small stain."

Yes, something was very wrong with this attempted sale. But what was the problem?

Risk.

"Fear of the unknown" kept prospects from buying this parachute.

Many times, the key to getting prospects to buy our products or join our business is simply the removal of risk. Instead of piling on more benefits, we should concentrate on removing the risk of failure that worries our prospects.

When two people decide to do business with each other, one person will have to assume the risk.

This person might be risking money, or their time. Risk causes fear and procrastination.

Want to make selling and sponsoring easier?

Let's give our prospects confidence by removing as much risk as possible.

Most companies offer some sort of money-back guarantee. Instead of just mentioning this guarantee, why not feature the guarantee? Why not make this risk-free guarantee a way to gain our prospects' confidence and trust?

If our prospects say, "I need to think it over," or delay making a decision, try removing the risk as our solution.

Here is an example of what we could say:

"Enroll tonight. All I ask you to do is set four or five appointments each week for the next four weeks. I will do the presentations. You watch. At the end of four weeks, we will evaluate our progress. If you are happy with the direction of your business, congratulations! You are part of the team. And if you are not happy with the direction of your business, the company will refund the entire cost of your distributor kit. You will have lost nothing."

Who could resist an offer like that?

No risk. No stress. No buyer's remorse.

How will our prospects feel about our guarantee now? They will appreciate the no-risk approach that made their decision easy.

When we remove risk for our prospects, decisions are easy. Our prospects don't have to worry if they made a bad decision. They won't have to worry if the bonus percentage is 10% or 11%. And they won't have to worry if they fail.

This removal of risk sounds like a pretty good idea. Let's look at this concept more closely in the next chapter.

REMOVING THE RISK.

Remember the big concept from the last chapter?

When two people decide to do business with each other, one person will have to assume the risk.

This person might be risking their money, or their time. Risk causes fear and procrastination.

Let's see how we feel when someone removes the risk for us.

A salesman asks us to buy a vacuum cleaner. The salesman assumes no risk. He gets money. On the other hand, **we** assume all the risk. We don't know if the vacuum cleaner will work as well as it did in the demonstration. We don't know if it will be easy to get service or parts. We don't know if the company will stand behind its guarantee if our vacuum cleaner breaks.

Since we must assume all the risk, we will want to "think it over" or check with other purchasers before making our decision to buy. If we must take all the risk, we want to be sure of our decision.

When we attempt to sponsor a new distributor, who takes all the risk?

The prospect.

We get our $100 for the distributor kit. There is no money out of our pockets.

However, our prospect must assume all the risk of this transaction. The prospect wonders if he can really build a business, if the training is sufficient, if the product guarantee will be honored, if we will help as much as we promised, etc., etc., etc.

That is why our prospects may be hesitant, want to "think it over," or decide not to take the risk. This makes prospects decline our invitations to become distributors.

The secret to successful closing is the "removal of risk."

If we reduce or remove the risk, our prospects will feel comfortable, and making the decision to become a distributor will be easy.

So how do we remove the risk?

Here are some ideas.

#1. Trial period.

Tell our hesitant prospect that becoming a distributor requires a seven-day probationary period. Our prospect must return the distributor kit and products for a full refund at the end of the seven days, or ... reaffirm his distributor agreement to become a permanent distributor.

This sounds better than a money-back guarantee to the prospect. It feels like a seven-day trial period with no obligation. This gives us seven days to educate our new distributor on the benefits of the products, help him sponsor some distributors, and start building an irresistible business.

What's another way to remove risk?

#2. Delaying the payment.

Try saying this to the nervous prospect.

"We won't charge your credit card for seven days. On day #7, you and I will meet. Then you can decide if our business is for you. If our business isn't for you, you don't lose anything. We cancel your agreement, and part as friends. If you love our business, then we will process your payment and activate the distributor agreement. Fair enough?"

Again, the prospect feels better as we take all the risk.

Another way to remove the risk?

#3. Incredible support.

Do we offer our help to a new distributor? Do we, or our sponsors, offer free training?

If we do, reposition these training sessions as "paid" training sessions. Then offer the sessions "free of charge" to our new distributor.

For example, we could say the following to our prospect:

"When you join our business, you take no risk. Why? Because our success team will meet you more than half-way. When you purchase your $100 starter kit, you receive all the manuals, videos, and audios. You will also receive a $150 scholarship to the Success Team's Power Training Course.

Over four consecutive Saturdays, you will learn from the highest earners in our business. You can't fail with our expert help."

If our new distributor attends the four Saturday training courses, he will have plenty of skills to earn a bonus check that will exceed the cost of his starter kit.

Wouldn't we love to have every new distributor faithfully attend training for four Saturdays in a row?

What is another way to remove risk?

#4. Stop talking about our personal success.

I get calls from prospects asking for advice. Many times, they ask:

"I think I will join this great company. My sponsor or upline makes $20,000 a month, so it must be a great opportunity. What do you think?"

My answer?

"How much your sponsor or upline makes doesn't mean a thing ... unless they offer to share their check with you. If only one person makes a big check, it doesn't mean everybody who joins will earn the same. You should have a better reason to be excited about your business. Can you think of some other great benefits?"

Why do I ask these prospects to refocus their thinking on the core benefits of their business? Because there are several ways to earn a big check.

First, we could front-load huge product packs on new, unsuspecting distributors and get a one-time big bonus check. Then, make copies of that check, and show that check for the next five years. Can our new prospect do the same thing? Hopefully not.

Second, we might have many years of successful experience in network marketing. For some reason, we decide to join a new company and bring our loyal downline and customers with us. We can then stand at the front of an opportunity meeting and say how we made thousands of dollars in our very first month. But can our new prospect with no previous experience do the same? Not likely.

Third, we might have a terrific personal warm market. Maybe we are the mayor of the city, own all the houses, and we simply ask our tenants to join. Sure, we will be off to a fast start, but can our new prospect duplicate this? Not likely.

Thinking it through.

I got a call from a new distributor who said:

"My upline makes $80,000 a month. I know this is a great company. Look at how much money I can earn!"

My response?

Big Al: Is this person the top earner in your company?

New Distributor: Yes, he is.

Big Al: So, there is no one else earning this much with this company. Only him, right?

New Distributor: Uh, right.

Big Al: And how many distributors are in this leader's downline?

New Distributor: About 90,000 distributors.

Big Al: What you are saying is that only one person out of 90,000 people earns $80,000 a month. And that 89,999 people fail to earn $80,000 a month, right?

New Distributor: Uh, uh, right.

Big Al: With odds of 89,999 to one, don't you think that planning your future based on those long, long odds is a bit dangerous?

New Distributor: Ouch. You are right. It doesn't matter how much my upline makes. What matters is what I can make, right?

Big Al: Right. And can your upline teach you the skills necessary to build a large and successful downline organization?

New Distributor: I am sure he can. After all, he has made some pretty good money.

Big Al: How often will this superstar leader call you, visit with you, train and help you?

New Distributor: Uh, never. He said at the opportunity meeting that he doesn't even return phone calls. He only talks to leaders at the Diamond Executive level.

Big Al: What's wrong with this picture?

New Distributor: Looks like I can't get any training or help until after I am successful. If I am already successful, well, I guess I wouldn't need any help then. But I can't become successful until I get training. Oh, this isn't going to work very well, is it?

Big Al: I am sure you can get some help from someone in your upline. You don't have to get help from the most successful person. In fact, being sponsored by a busy leader is sometimes a disadvantage. Why? Because this leader must share his limited time with 90,000 people. Try to find someone in your upline who can give you some help. You will need to learn the skills to be successful if you are going to earn the monthly income you want.

The real question the distributor should be asking is:

"Can my sponsor teach me the skills to build a large and successful downline organization?"

It is not what the superstar leader earns that counts. It is what the new prospect can earn that counts.

What is the point of this story?

This is why we shouldn't talk about our personal success. What we earn doesn't matter. It doesn't remove risk for our prospect.

Instead, talk about other people we have sponsored and how they have experienced success in our business.

You see, our prospect wants to know if we can teach him the skills to be successful.

When we talk about the other people we have helped, our new prospect gains confidence. He feels that we are a "success-maker" and that we won't abandon him when he joins. Listening to stories of how we have helped others builds our prospect's confidence … and helps removes his risk.

We might say:

"Let me tell you about Mary Jones. When I sponsored her last year, she told me she wanted to build a successful business. I accompanied her to the trainings, helped her with presentations, and did three-way calls with her group when she was vacationing in Hawaii. Now, Mary is more successful than I am. She quit her job and moved her family to a new house just outside of the city limits.

"And then there is Joe Smith. Joe wanted a part-time income to help pay off his credit cards. We figured that with an extra $225 a month, he could pay off his credit cards in about two years. Well, Joe and I did some retail presentations and got some referrals. Now his retail profits exceed $300 a month. Plus, Joe gets an extra bonus check for $100 - $200 a month. Joe loves his job and will continue working part-time with us. However, now he can afford to keep his job and have his credit cards paid off too.

"And let me tell you about Jane Doe. She started with us about two years ago just so she could buy her products at wholesale. After a couple of her friends at work asked her to order some products, Jane changed her mind. She asked me if I would help her build a part-time business. Jane and I did some home parties, talked with several of her friends, and we did mini-trainings with several of her groups. Now, Jane is still part-time with our company. But, she earned her first bonus car and her average take-home earnings are about $1,500 a month."

After listening to these stories, what is our prospect thinking?

He is thinking,

"Wow! If you sponsor me in this business, you will help me become successful. You helped others become successful. There is no risk for me if I put forth the effort. And I will put forth extra effort now that I know I am guaranteed success with your help."

Look at it this way. We don't care what the head of our government earns. He or she isn't going to share that paycheck with us. But, if we were considering a government cabinet post, we would be interested in how much money the other cabinet officials earn.

Remember, the crucial factor in sponsoring a new distributor revolves around this principle:

When two people decide to do business with each other, one person will have to assume the risk.

Our job is to remove as much of that risk as possible for our prospect.

GIVE OUR PROSPECTS THE "TRUTH" GUARANTEE.

Prospects are afraid to take risks. That is only natural. As humans, we focus on survival. That is a primary program in our minds.

So when prospects resist, network marketers attempt to soothe their fears by saying things such as:

- "Try our business. We have a 30-day money-back guarantee."

- "Try our product or service. We have a 30-day money-back guarantee."

Did you ever notice that these guarantees seldom close our prospects?

Why? Because many prospects feel embarrassed taking advantage of a refund. So, they never make the initial commitment to try the product, service, or business opportunity.

Why not try this? Give our prospects the "truth" guarantee. It will shock our prospects and create a "fear of loss" motivation. Say:

"I have one guarantee about our business. If you don't try anything, you are guaranteed that nothing will change. The commute time to your job won't change. The limited time you have with your family won't change. Your current paycheck won't change."

And now our prospects must think. They realize that saying "no" would be giving up all hope of a solution.

A little humor.

The prospects asked the network marketer, "Is there a guarantee? Will you guarantee that we will make money and be successful in this business?"

The network marketer replied,

"First, you will have to invest $150,000. Plus, you will have to train for four consecutive years at no pay. You will miss your salary during these four years. Finally, at the end of these four years, there is no guarantee that you will have a job.

"Oh wait! My fault. I was describing a college education by mistake."

Okay, of course we can't say that to prospects, but a little humor makes learning so much easier.

Misdirection.

One way to handle objections is to re-direct the conversation to what really matters. It is easier to answer an objection when we set the rules about what is important.

Here is how that works. We take our prospect's current objection, and minimize it. Now the objection is not an important element in the final decision. Then, we direct our prospect's attention to the big question, the real question we want our prospect to answer.

This is easier to see in the following story.

"Guess who has the best product in network marketing?"

About 30 years ago, I gave a presentation. I told the prospect how my company had the best vitamins ever with more milligrams than the competition. The prospect should join my company because we had the best product!

My friend, Tom Paredes came with me to watch my presentation. He couldn't wait to poke fun at me later.

After the presentation, Tom and I were eating Mexican food at an all-you-can-eat buffet. Tom turns to me and tells me this story.

Imagine you join my company because my product has 100 milligrams of Vitamin C. It is the best product out there. You make your list, you sign up a few distributors and create a few customers.

But three weeks later, a brand-new company starts and their product has 101 milligrams of Vitamin C. It is better. So, what do you have to do if you want to represent the best product?

Quit.

You apologize to your distributors. You make a refund to your customers. Then you join Company B because they have the "best" product.

You make your list, you sign up a few distributors and create a few customers.

But three weeks later, a brand-new company starts. Their product has 102 milligrams of Vitamin C. It is better. So, what do you have to do if you want to represent the best product?

Quit.

You apologize to your distributors. You make a refund to your customers. Then you join Company C because they have the "best" product.

But three weeks later, a brand-new company starts and their product has 103 milligrams of Vitamin C plus … a much cooler brochure. Everything is better. So, what do you have to do if you want to represent the best product?

Quit.

You can never build a long-term residual income if you start over every three weeks.

◇◇◇◇

Ouch. Tom was right.

But he didn't stop there. He couldn't resist rubbing it in a little more.

Tom did the same story about compensation plans. He told me how I would have to switch every time a new company came out with a different percentage on level three, etc.

And after Tom finished re-directing my attention away from the "who or what is best" issue, he told me what to say next.

He said, "So the real question is, do you want to build a long-term residual income now or not?"

And that is how I learned my lesson.

We must make decisions on the things that count.

If we try to sponsor people by talking about our wonderful product or compensation plan, we open ourselves up to comparisons and objections. Not good.

But we can re-direct the prospect's thoughts to issues such as:

1.   Do I want to be in business or not?

2. Do I want to be in business with this person or not?

3. Am I ready to do something for my family now ... or not?

4. Can you teach me the skills to build a large and successful network marketing business?

If we do this, then we don't have to answer minor objections. The prospect can concentrate on the big picture.

It is easier to sponsor people based on what we can do for them.

Stop arguing facts.

We want to change our habits of quoting facts and statistics, and create a new future by doing something different.

Think about it this way. Does it matter to the prospect if 41% of the ingredients came from China instead of 53%?

No.

What matters is if they want to create a successful business ... and if we can show them how. That is their real issue.

So we will re-direct our prospects' questions and objections to one of these final questions:

1. Do I want to be in business or not?

2. Do I want to be in business with this person or not?

3. Am I ready to do something for my family now ... or not?

4. Can you teach me the skills to build a large and successful network marketing business?

Now we can move forward with our prospects to help them start their businesses.

INSIDE THE MINDS OF OUR PROSPECTS.

Our prospects' current state of mind is key to getting "yes" decisions. Think about it this way. If our prospects feel agitated, worried, or upset, our chances of getting a "yes" decision diminish. We must be aware of our prospects' moods.

Sometimes this is outside our control. Maybe a prospect gets an upsetting phone call during our presentation. Or, maybe an emergency arises while we are presenting our program. In these cases, it is best to come back and resume later. With almost no chance of getting a "yes" decision, it's likely our next visit will have better odds.

The likeability factor.

We should also check how our prospects feel toward us.

Prospects love to do business with people they know, like, and trust. Have we earned this from our prospects?

No matter how good our offer, if our prospects don't feel connected with us, they will find someone else with a similar offer. What can we do to increase our likeability factor?

The most obvious things we should do are:

1. Smile. When we smile, other people naturally react by smiling back. This is a great first step.

2. Don't argue or correct our prospects. Only in extreme cases should we disagree with them, and only on the most important points. Nobody likes people who disagree with them. We can save our opinions for another time.

3. Be a great listener. Prospects love people who listen. If we do all the talking, our prospects will become stressed, waiting for their turn to talk.

4. Compliment our prospects. Sincerely compliment them on at least one thing.

5. Be respectful of our prospects' choices. They have to live with the choices they make. Remember, we are there only to add one more option to their lives.

THE CONTRAST CLOSE.

Here is a way to handle price objections. The price objection could be about the cost of our product, our service, or the cost to join our business.

If we get price objections from our prospects, we will want to be more preemptive in handling this objection. We can get our prospects to agree that our price is fair … before we announce our final price.

How can we do this? My friend, Bernie De Souza, is a master of the contrast principle. He manages the price and value expectations of his prospects in two easy steps.

Step #1. Make the benefit of our business or product as big as possible in our prospects' minds. For example, state how much our prospects could earn in one year, two years or even three years. Or, how expensive it would be to personally locate and buy individual ingredients for a health product.

Step #2. Then, ask our prospects, "If you had a business or product that could deliver this benefit, how much would you expect to pay for that business or product?"

Then, give our prospects three choices.

Choice A: A really high number.

Choice B: A ridiculously low number.

Choice C: A number that is reasonable, but appears to be a bargain.

This is easier to demonstrate with an example. In this example, let's imagine that it costs $100 to get started in our business opportunity. The conversation with a prospect would go something like this.

Us: Even if this business only earns you $500 a month, in three years that would be $18,000 in your pocket. If you had a business that earned you $18,000, how much would you expect to invest to get started in that business?

A. $10,000?

B. $10?

C. $100?

Prospects will pick the third choice almost every time. They will say, "$100." And we can reply, "Sounds about right."

Yes, all we have to do is agree with them.

We can use the same contrast principle to talk about the price of a product, service, or even a convention ticket. Let's do a quick example for our company's convention ticket.

Us: Our company convention is the highlight of our year. Not only will we meet important and inspiring people, but the company pays for the convention hall, the meals, and also gives us new samples. Even if the motivation and information from our company convention only earns you an extra $100 a month, that's $1,200 more in your pocket in 12 months. How much would you expect to pay for a ticket to get all the meals, training, samples, and education?

A. $10,000?

B. $10?

C. $200?

As usual, people will pick the third number almost every time. They will say, "$200." And we can reply, "Sounds about right."

Remember these keys.

Create value in what we offer, then give our prospects three choices.

Choice A: A really high number.

Choice B: A ridiculously low number.

Choice C: A number that is reasonable, but appears to be a bargain.

And then agree when they choose Choice C.

CURIOSITY KILLED THE CAT.

This old saying is true. Curiosity is a strong, strong motivator.

About 45 years ago, I attended an opportunity meeting as a guest of a friend. The speaker knew how to use curiosity as a close to get prospects to step forward, and make a commitment.

This is what the speaker did.

As the meeting progressed, the speaker turned page after page from his presentation flipchart. Each page had a better benefit than the page before. Everyone wanted to join as a distributor.

Suddenly the speaker stopped and said:

"Folks, as you can see, there is much, much more to our opportunity. But I am not allowed to show you the good stuff. We only reveal the good stuff to distributors who commit to becoming SuperExecutives.

"If you want to be a SuperExecutive, you have to do this. You have to call your boss and tell him that you won't be at work tomorrow morning. Then, you will come back here for a special three-hour training where we will reveal the big secret. You will learn how to earn the big money you always wanted."

I looked around the room. Some guests shuffled their feet, but most of the guests had fire in their eyes. They couldn't wait until tomorrow morning. They wanted to learn the insider secrets, the trade secrets, the big money plan and more.

No one had to close the prospects in that room.

A strong close? Yes.

Is this the close we want to use? Maybe, or maybe not. But it is one additional close that may be appropriate in certain situations.

Not every close works for everyone, in every situation, and for every prospect. We want to have a large inventory of closes that we can choose from.

Objections:
The big picture.

Our prospects want to join, but they also want more assurance. They have never participated in our business before, or have never tried our products. Understandably, they could be a bit nervous about the future.

But many times, our prospects want to make a "yes" decision, and that is why they ask for more assurances by voicing objections. If they had no interest in our offer, we wouldn't be talking now.

Think about this. We talk to a salesman. We have no interest in the salesman's offer. Would we ask more questions and voice more objections to prolong the presentation torture? Of course not. We would want to finish the conversation as quickly as possible and leave.

Look on the bright side. Objections mean that our prospects want to join. They just want a little bit more assurance before making that final "yes" decision.

Why do prospects have objections?

Here are some common reasons prospects hesitate when we ask for a decision:

1. Our prospects don't want what we offer. They would rather spend their money on something else.

2. Our prospects don't need what we offer. They feel that they wouldn't use our products. Or, our opportunity is something that they wouldn't want.

3. Our prospects are content where they are. Life is good. No need to change anything.

4. Our prospects have another solution in mind. They think our solution is inferior. Someone else made a better, more compelling offer.

5. Our prospects hate change. They feel that change opens up the possibility for mistakes. They would rather keep their current situation than risk trying something new.

6. Our prospects don't have the money. They have already spent their money on another offer.

7. Our prospects don't have the authority to make decisions. They must talk to their boss, their spouse, or someone else for permission to make a decision.

We need to know these things.

In the minds of our prospects, these reasons are legitimate. These are real reasons that create real objections.

We must address these objections confidently. Why?

Because prospects need assurance.

As we mentioned earlier, prospects will have to commit to their next step with a bit of faith. Remember, our prospects haven't tried our products or our opportunity. Will they feel a bit nervous and insecure? Certainly.

If we are not confident, they won't want to join us. They won't want to accompany us on our journey if they think they are going to die with us on the way. They want us to have rock-solid confidence that their journey will be successful.

To put ourselves in our prospects' shoes, let's use the following example.

The doctor visit.

Our doctor says, "I am not sure which course of treatment you should take. Maybe we could try this one ... or I don't know, this one might have a chance of working also."

How would we feel about this doctor's lack of confidence? We would be running to a new doctor. If our doctor was not confident, we would avoid his advice.

It is the same in network marketing. Our prospects desperately look for someone to follow. But that "someone to follow" needs to display confidence.

What we shouldn't say to prospects.

"I'm trying this business. Hope I will do well. Do you want to join?"

Okay, that is not exactly what we say, but that may be what our prospects hear.

Most prospects are followers. They don't want to follow someone who is not committed to their destination. They don't want to waste their time following someone who is going to turn back.

We must assure our prospects that we will do whatever it takes to get to our destination. That will make the decision to follow us easier.

Now, let's look at some common objections in the next chapter.

COMMON OBJECTIONS.

Objections are not that difficult. If we are in this business long enough, we will notice that there are only a few common objections. These objections will come up again and again. All we need to do is figure out how to answer them one time. Then we can use our answers over and over again.

In the beginning, we fear objections much more than we need to. Remember, objections mean that our prospects are still interested.

The first rule of objections?

Agree.

The best way to handle objections is to agree with the objection first.

An objection may be valid to our prospects. We don't know what has happened in their lives. We don't know the events that caused this objection. We don't know which programs our prospects received from their parents, teachers, the news, and their associations with others.

It's possible that the objection has merit. And then again, maybe not. Our prospects want us to listen. And by agreeing to the objection, we show our prospects that we care about their thoughts.

If we disagree with our prospects, we cut off all communication. While we are disagreeing, our prospects are thinking of reasons to support their position. Since the conscious human mind can only do one thing at a time, this means our prospects are not listening to us. Yes, that means we are talking, and no one is listening.

The solution? We must agree with our prospects first. Then, communication can continue.

Books are written on this. Verbal combat, backing prospects into corners, and pressuring friends are not the best ways to build relationships with your future team. So, what should we do?

First, acknowledge that we heard the objection. Next, agree with our prospects' point of view.

Agree???

Yes, agree. If we argue, our prospects aren't listening. Our prospects are thinking of what they will say next to support their position. We can't win arguments, but if we agree with our prospects, then there is no argument.

We will use these words.

- "Relax."
- "It is okay."
- "Of course."
- "Yes, I see."
- "Correct."

These words stop the drama inside our prospects' minds. This means our prospects can listen to what we say next instead of thinking of more proof for their position.

Now, two-way communication can begin.

Let's look at the most common objections.

Our prospect says, "I don't have any time."

What should we do?

Agree. We can answer that objection with, "Of course you don't have any time. That is exactly why I am talking with you now. You don't want this to be true for the rest of your life. Let's discuss some possibilities now, so that you will never be in this situation again."

What?

What happened here?

In 10 seconds, we took an objection and turned it into a, "Yes, let's see how this can work."

Magic? No. Here is exactly what we did.

"Of course you don't have any time."

When we open with this phrase, our prospect relaxes. In his mind, he reasons, "I don't have to think of any more objections. You agree with me. There is no need for me to keep my defenses up for this conversation to continue. Well, since I don't have to think of anything to support my current position, what am I going to do? I guess I might as well listen to what you are going to say."

There is no communication unless our prospect has an open mind. The first rule of handling objections is to agree with the objection. If there is conflict, our prospect will be thinking about ideas to support his position. Since the conscious mind can only have one thought at a time, that means our prospect will not be hearing a word we say.

While we would rather argue our position, it is much better for us to agree. Now, at least we have an audience for our message.

"That is why I am talking with you now."

Remember the magic of rapport? We can build better rapport by telling our prospect a fact that he already believes. When we say we are talking with him now, the back of his mind says, "Yes, you're telling the truth. You are talking with me now. I can believe what you're saying."

"You don't want this to be true for the rest of your life."

Again, we tell our prospect a fact that he already believes. Of course he wants his life to be different. He doesn't enjoy being too busy. Now what is our prospect thinking? "Yes, you're telling the truth. I don't want to be busy for the rest of my life. I can believe what you say." After these two facts, our prospect has a more open mind that will allow our message to enter.

"Let's discuss some possibilities now, so that you will never be in this situation again."

This is the message we wanted to deliver. We want our prospect to accept our offer of helping him figure out a solution. The previous sentences in our answer had one purpose. To open our prospect's mind, so he could listen and accept this message.

Because our prospect accepted this message, he has already made up his mind that he wants to join. It is now a matter of sorting out some time issues. This is a great example of taking an objection and, in only 10 seconds, turning the objection into a positive decision to move forward.

You want something stronger?

Our prospect complains, "I don't have any time!"

We reply, "Of course you don't have any time. All 24 hours of your day are used up already. So what are you willing to sacrifice in your day so that you can change your family's future?"

Yes, a lot stronger and probably not appropriate for most prospects. But for some prospects, it might be the right thing to say to move them forward.

Before we go further, let's take a moment to explain the rapport skill mentioned above.

Prospects have fears. Their survival programs are on full alert during sales presentations. They think, "What is the catch? There is always a catch!"

Because prospects are skeptical, our messages get filtered, modified, and many times rejected. Ouch. When prospects don't believe us, even the best presentation is wasted.

To reduce skepticism and build a better relationship, we should start our conversations with facts our prospects already believe. This establishes trust. Now getting our message through to our prospects becomes easier.

What can we say that our prospects already believe? How about something like this:

- We all want to live longer.
- Wrinkles are overrated.
- We want longer weekends.
- It would be great to fire the boss.
- We need more vacation time.
- Looking good is important.
- Dying early is inconvenient.
- Electric bills are so high.

See the bonding potential? Now our message will have a better chance of entering our prospects' brains.

Okay, enough about the rapport technique.

Back to objections. Could a version of this objection formula work for other objections?

Yes. Let's try a few now. While these won't work for every objection, we can use them for a few common objections.

"I don't have any money."

Yes, our prospect is pleading poverty.

Prospect: "I can't afford $49 for a distributor kit."

Sponsor: "You have cable television, right? Which will make you more money? Cable television or our opportunity?"

If our prospect doesn't subscribe to cable television, just modify our answer. Instead, mention another typical expense such as:

- Smoking.
- Beer.
- Golf.
- Eating at restaurants.
- Movies.
- Pizza.
- Manicures.

But, instead of this answer, why not use the formula we just learned? Let's see how that would sound.

"I don't have any money."

What should we say? This is going to be easy.

"Of course you don't have any money. That is why I am talking with you now. You don't want to be that way for the rest of your life. So let's sit down now and figure out a way to get the money to get you started."

Remember the formula?

Did we agree with our prospect? Yes.

And look at the first three sentences. All three sentences state facts that build rapport. Our prospect can agree with us on these three facts. What is our prospect thinking? "You tell the truth. We agree on things. I can listen to you with an open mind."

And the final sentence? "So let's sit down now and figure out a way to get the money to get you started." This final sentence guides our prospect into a discussion on how to finance his business. By having this discussion, the prospect has assumed a "yes" decision. Otherwise this discussion would be meaningless.

How do we get a prospect started who has no money to join? Well, that is not the purpose of this book. But motivated prospects who want to change their lives will figure out a way. Maybe they hold an advance meeting or two, or a product party, or take preorders, or sell that goofy lava lamp that has been sitting in the garage for 40+ years. We can certainly help with the plan for financing, now that our prospect has made the decision to join.

"Your product is too expensive."

Try saying this:

"Our product is a treat or luxury. It is sort of like spending money on dining out, having a manicure, lottery tickets, or beer."

If our prospects spend money on these things, they can afford our product.

We can make up our own list of appropriate luxuries that our prospects might be spending money on now.

"I don't know anyone."

We should recognize a pattern by now.

"Of course you don't know anyone. That is why I am talking with you now. You don't want that to be the case for the rest of your life. That is why the company has a special training program that will show you how to meet new, positive people. Plus, you will have me as a sponsor to help out. So let's sit down now and get you started, so we can get you enrolled in the company training program right away."

The above objection response should need no explanation.

Let's try another objection.

"I don't know how to do this type of business."

"Of course you don't know how to do this type of business. No one expects us to know how to work a business before we start. That would be silly. That is why the company has a special training program that helps us get started even if we have zero knowledge. Plus, you will have me as your sponsor to help you every step of the way. So let's sit down now and get you started, so we can get you enrolled in the company training program right away."

One more?

"I am not a salesman."

"Of course you are not a salesman. That is why I am talking with you now. The company doesn't want a bunch of old-school, sleazy, door-to-door salespeople promoting its products. They want real people, just like you and me, to share our experiences with others. So let's sit down now and get you started. Because, as a non-salesperson, this opportunity is made for people like you and me."

But aren't there other types of objections?

Sure. But most objections just reflect uncertainty. Prospects want to feel better about their decision to join. Here is an example.

Do you have a refrigerator?

My friend, Mike Lewis, tells this story that answers the "saturation objection."

Prospect: But what about saturation? After a while, everyone will have bought or joined and there will be no one to sell to.

Mike: Do you have a refrigerator?

Prospect: Yes. Everybody has a refrigerator.

Mike: How many stores sell refrigerators in your city?

Prospect: There are a lot of stores that sell refrigerators in my city.

Mike: Refrigerators last for 10, 15, or even 20 years, right? Yet the stores have been selling refrigerators for a long, long time. And these stores do very well.

Prospect: Oh.

The big objection.

Did you notice that one big objection is missing here in this chapter? This objection is so big that we will devote an entire chapter to it. What is this objection?

"I want to think it over."

This objection haunts and frustrates network marketers. But we will get rid of that fear forever once we learn how to handle that objection. So let's get on with the next chapter.

"I WANT TO THINK IT OVER."

This will be a long chapter. Why?

Because prospects love to say:

- "I want to think it over."
- "I will let you know."
- "I will keep it in mind."
- "Let me get back to you on this."
- "We need more time to discuss this."
- "I have to check with someone first."

At workshops, I say this to the women. "Ladies, give me your honest feedback on this. Please tell me what you really mean when a man calls you for a dinner date, and you reply, 'I need to think it over.'"

The men let out a slightly uncomfortable laugh. The women laugh loudly and in unison reply, "No."

So I ask the women, "Why don't you tell the man 'No' directly?"

They reply, "Because we don't want to hurt the man's feelings. We are polite."

We should take a hint.

When our prospects tell us, "I need to think it over," what should we think?

"No."

In most cases our prospects are being polite. They want to help us "save face" and avoid embarrassment. It doesn't take a rocket scientist to translate their reply as a rejection of our offer. We too should take a hint.

Plus, our prospect doesn't want to argue or have an objection war. Our prospect just wants to get out of this uncomfortable situation.

If we sense this, let's accept that our offer isn't for these prospects. We can keep our good relationships with people by also being polite.

But ... but ... but ...

Okay, we are thinking, "Sure. Many times our prospects are telling us they are not interested."

But sometimes they really do want what we offer, but don't have the courage to make that final decision. What should we, as professionals, do to help them?

Reversing the "I want to think it over" objection.

People are afraid of making decisions. Our employers train us not to make decisions. They want us to come to work for them, but they don't want us to think. They just want us to follow instructions.

Imagine that I work as a cashier at a fast-food restaurant. You come in and say, "I want a hamburger with pickles on one side."

As the cashier, I think, "Well, if I put pickles on one side, will I get a raise?"

No. There is no upside or benefit for me in honoring your request. Plus, if I don't follow the standard procedure by putting pickles on both sides, I could get fired. There is a tremendous downside or penalty for me if I make a decision based on your request.

So what will I do? I will say, "It is just not possible. I have to put pickles on both sides."

Yes, our bosses train us to not make decisions.

And what if we make a bad decision?

Here is the second reason we don't want to make decisions.

Have we ever made bad decisions in the past? Yes. And how did we feel when we made those bad decisions? Bad.

Oh, and we've made so many bad decisions in our lives. For example, remember when we had that opportunity to buy stock in that fast-growing company and we didn't? Later we kicked ourselves in regret. Or, we looked at a house or property and thought it was too expensive. Ten years later we realized our mistake. The property appreciated beyond our wildest expectations. Yes, our bad decisions stick with us.

And what happens when we think about those bad decisions again? We feel bad. Over our lifetime, we may rethink bad decisions 1,000 times or more. We get the same bad feeling each time we remember our bad decisions.

Over time, our subconscious minds say, "Don't you ever make another decision again. It may turn out bad. Then we will feel bad over and over again."

This is why people hate making decisions. This is why we put off decisions as long as possible.

However, the reality is that we are always making decisions. We have to make hundreds or thousands of decisions every hour. Our body automatically makes 100,000 decisions every second just to keep us alive. These automatic decisions are easy. We don't have to think about them.

But what about those decisions we <u>do</u> think about?

We hate those decisions. We don't want to make decisions, but we have to.

When we put off or delay making a decision … we are actually making a decision to keep our current circumstances!

Here is an example of not making a decision.

I am sitting here eating ice cream. Spoonful after spoonful after spoonful. You ask me, "Why don't you make a decision to diet?"

And I say, "Yes, that is something I should think about." Meanwhile I continue shoveling spoonful after spoonful of ice cream into my mouth. What does this mean?

It means that I made a decision. "No, I will not make a decision to diet now. I am enjoying this ice cream. I will continue to eat ice cream. And that is my final decision!"

Want another example?

I stand in the middle of a busy highway. Trucks are speeding towards me. I think, "I need to make a decision. Should I run off to the right? Or run off to the left?"

But, I decide not to make a decision.

Well, tragedy approaches. Not making a decision to run off the highway ... is making a decision to stay where I am. That decision will be costly.

Whoa! So there is no such thing as "thinking it over" in real life!

Here is the reality.

We make a decision to move forward and change, or we make a decision to stay where we are.

We know this. Prospects don't.

So we have to tell them!

Then our prospects will realize that they cannot put off decisions until later.

Their choices?

Either make a decision to stay where they are without our products, services, or opportunity ... or to move forward with us.

Now our prospects understand that "not making a decision" is actually "making a decision to keep their current circumstances."

Our prospects can no longer use the "I need to think it over" objection.

Prospects make a decision to keep their problems, or work with us.

Procrastination?

Prospects hate making decisions. They are afraid of making a wrong decision. So what do they do?

They pretend to delay the decision by saying that they need to think it over.

All we have to do is tell them:

"You can make a decision to start today. Or, you can make a decision not to start today, and keep your life exactly like it is right now."

This helps prospects realize that there is always a decision. Delaying is a decision to refuse our offer and keep their circumstances the same.

But saying this is too direct. We don't want to upset our prospects. So, we will use better words to convey this message.

How do we say this?

Start with this simple phrase: "Relax, it is okay ..."

When our prospects hear these words, they will think this. "Wow. You agreed with me. I can relax. I don't have to think of excuses to support my objection. I like people who agree with me. So, please continue."

At this moment, our prospects have opened their minds. We can continue our conversation.

Next, we will tell our prospects that it is okay to make a decision not to buy or not to join. This alerts them to the fact that not moving forward is a decision to stay where they are. Here are some examples.

- "Relax, it is okay to make a decision not to join our business tonight."
- "Relax, it is okay to make a decision not to purchase these vitamins tonight."
- "Relax, it is okay to make a decision to keep your current utility supplier."
- "Relax, it is okay to make a decision not to purchase our hydrating night cream tonight."

We are polite. We have honored our prospects' decisions.

But there is more.

All decisions have consequences.

We should point out the consequences of our prospects' decisions to stay where they are. Let's add consequences to these four examples.

- "Relax, it is okay to make a decision not to join our business tonight, and continue commuting two hours each way to a job that you hate."
- "Relax, it is okay to make a decision not to purchase these vitamins tonight, and continue to let your body feel older and older every day."

135

- "Relax, it is okay to make a decision to keep your current utility supplier, and continue paying the highest utility rates on your street."

- "Relax, it is okay to make a decision not to purchase our hydrating night cream tonight, and continue to listen to your skin wrinkle every night when you go to sleep."

Now our prospects know they made a choice.

That was easy, wasn't it?

We acknowledged their choice. Suddenly, our prospects realize that "thinking it over" is really a choice not to buy or not to join. "Thinking it over" is a choice to keep their current circumstances. That is all we want to do, let them know it was a choice.

And there are terrible consequences in keeping their current circumstances.

Here are a few examples of what happens when prospects make the decision to stay where they are:

- Having to work longer at a job they hate.

- Having to waking up to an alarm clock for the rest of their lives.

- Placing their children in daycare instead of having them at home.

- Having a limited income opportunity with their fixed-income jobs.

- Delaying the type of holidays and memories they want.

- Hoping that the company pension will be enough.

Thinking it over is expensive. Let's make sure our prospects know the real cost of not moving forward. We provide a disservice to prospects if we do not alert them to the consequences of keeping their lives the same. Our prospects should feel the urgency of acting now.

But there is more!

While we have our prospects' attention, we can remind our prospects of the benefits of moving forward with us. Here is how that will sound:

- "Relax, it is okay to make a decision not to join our business tonight, and continue commuting two hours each way to a job that you hate. But, it is also okay to make a decision to start tonight, so we can start the countdown to firing your boss."

- "Relax, it is okay to make a decision not to purchase these vitamins tonight, and continue letting your body feel older and older every day. But, it is also okay to make a decision to start taking care of your body tonight, so you will have that energy you want for quality family time."

- "Relax, it is okay to make a decision to keep your current utility supplier, and continue paying the highest utility rates on your street. But, it is also okay to get online now for 10 minutes, and start paying lower utility rates like everyone else."

- "Relax, it is okay to make a decision not to purchase our hydrating night cream tonight, and continue listening to your skin wrinkle every night. But, it is also okay to make a decision to put off those wrinkles an extra 15 years by protecting your skin with this cream."

Is there a formula for this?

Of course. Here it is:

"Relax, it is okay to make a decision not to [insert the "no" decision] and [insert consequences]. But is also okay to make a decision to [buy or join] and [insert benefits].

It is that easy.

Polite? Yes.

Rejection-free? Yes.

Forces prospects to give us a "yes" or "no" answer? Yes.

Done.

Exaggerated examples.

Exaggeration is a great memory technique. When we exaggerate things to a fantasy level, our minds recall it easily. Let's exaggerate these previous four examples. Of course, we would never use these exaggerations, but it is a fun memory exercise. Here they are.

- "Relax, it is okay to make a decision not to join our business tonight, and continue commuting two hours each way to work with a dream-sucking vampire boss who takes little bits of your brain out every day, turning you into a human zombie. But, it is also okay to make a decision to start tonight, so we can start the countdown to firing your boss."

- "Relax, it is okay to make a decision not to purchase these vitamins tonight, and save some money by choosing to die a little earlier. But, it is also okay to make a decision to start taking care of your body tonight, so you will have that energy you want for quality family time."

- "Relax, it is okay to make a decision to keep your current utility supplier, and continue paying the highest utility rates on your street, while your neighbors secretly laugh behind your back. But, it is also okay to get online now for 10 minutes, and start paying lower utility rates like everyone else."

- "Relax, it is okay to make a decision not to purchase our hydrating night cream tonight, and hope your new wrinkles give you the respect older people receive. But, it is also okay to make a decision to put off those wrinkles an extra 15 years by protecting your skin with this cream."

Is this the only way to handle the "I want to think it over" objection?

No. But it works well. Here are two other ways to handle this common objection.

As always, choose the way that is the most comfortable for you.

"Now, it is your time to choose."

This is a bit more direct. We are telling our prospects they must make a choice now. However, we are telling them to make their choice in a very polite way. They still feel they are in charge of their decisions.

By using the simple word "choose," we eliminate the natural response: "I need to think it over."

Will it remove this objection forever? No. But it will greatly reduce the number of times it comes up.

People like to choose. And what are the choices we give our prospects?

#1. Keeping their lives exactly as they are without the benefits of our products or opportunity.

#2. Improving their lives by taking advantage of our products or opportunity.

Not a tough choice to make. Most prospects will naturally choose choice #2.

Why would prospects choose choice #1? Why would prospects put off or delay having our benefits?

The answer is in our rapport and presentation steps. If we left unanswered questions there, prospects will feel uneasy about moving forward. However, if we did a great job creating rapport and presenting, most prospects will choose the obvious choice, #2.

Or, if you don't like using the "Now, it is your time to choose" close, you can reword it more elegantly with these two sentences:

"So, Mr. and Mrs. Prospect, you don't have to do anything, and things will remain the same. Or, if you are ready to change now, let's get started."

This is just a different way of reducing the chances of our prospects saying, "I need to think it over." Plus, we let our prospects know that we can get them started right now.

And finally, here is a third way to handle this objection.

Limit the choices.

If we give our prospect choices, don't include "I want to think it over" as one of the options. Provide choices such as:

1. Start now.

2. Start now with the big pack.

3. Become a customer.

4. No.

Most prospects will assume these are the only four choices, and will pick the choice that is appropriate for them.

IT ISN'T ALWAYS OUR FAULT.

"I need to think it over" comes up frequently in presentations.

Here is an example that shows that the problem wasn't created by us. This time, the prospects' own minds created the objection.

The end of our presentation.

We give our best presentation. And now it is time for the close.

We ask our prospect to join and our prospect says:

"Sounds great! Awesome! I would like to …"

And at that moment, something happens inside our prospect's mind. The conscious mind wants to join. It makes sense. More money, more freedom, great products. But remember, the conscious mind doesn't make decisions. It is only the size of a pea.

This is where the subconscious mind of our prospect steps in, taps the conscious mind on the shoulder and says:

"Uh, before we say that we want to join, consider this. I have been keeping track of our life. When we learned to walk, our brothers and sisters laughed at our failures. When we were four years old, we spilled our milk and our parents yelled at us. Our teachers pointed out all of our spelling mistakes. In high school, the other kids teased us and made fun of us. Our boss doesn't respect us, we constantly make mistakes ... and the score is: 1,231,457 votes that we are a loser. And, now this stranger is making one little vote saying that we could be a winner? Uh, I don't think so."

So now the conscious mind takes over and finishes our prospect's reply to our closing question by saying:

"Sounds great! Awesome! I would like to ... THINK IT OVER!"

Think it over???

Well, the prospect's conscious mind didn't want to say:

"Hey, I talked it over with my subconscious mind which runs my life. And my subconscious mind said the evidence was overwhelming that this would be just another failure in my life. Guess I am a full-time loser."

That reply would be embarrassing. So instead, the conscious mind "saves face" by telling us, "I would like to think it over."

This happens.

And when it does, we will have to work harder to give more guarantees and assurances to our nervous prospect.

MORE AND MORE INFORMATION.

We talk to a prospect, give our presentation, and then ask for a decision to move forward. And what does the prospect say?

"I need more information!"

What are we going to say next?

If this problem happens over and over again, are we going to be victims ... or master exactly what to say next?

Here is what we can do. We will re-focus our prospect back to the big question: "Do you want to start a business with me ... or not?"

We can say to our prospect, "If you enjoy gathering information, that is okay. But at some point, we will have to stop collecting information, stop putting off action, and take our first step forward to start our business. We can collect information for years after we start our business, but we need to start it first. So the real question that you and I have is this. Do you want to start a business now ... or not?"

It is difficult to fight a prospect's continuing need for more information. However, we can change the conversation from collecting information to, "Do I want to start now or not?"

Here is a slightly different way to approach this problem.

Stopping the stream of questions.

Prospects are nervous and unsure. To delay making a decision, they may resort to asking question after question after question. This doesn't eliminate our prospects' decision, but only puts it off.

Rather than answer unending trivial questions, consider this approach. The trivial questions could be answered with:

"That is covered in training. But the real question is, 'Do you want to join our business now, so that we can get you enrolled in training right away?'"

Our prospects should appreciate that we bring the focus back to the big question, "Do I want to start a business with you now, or not?"

If our prospects don't want to start now, then it doesn't matter how good our compensation plan pays on level 18.

It is over.

BE FAIR. SHOW PROSPECTS THEIR OPTIONS.

Indecision and doubt are our enemies. If our prospects feel that there might be a better solution in the future, they will not want to decide now. Why? Because they fear that the better option in the future will make any decision made right now look bad.

Doubt and fear are the basis of many objections. What can we do to eliminate this?

We could list the obvious solutions to our prospects' problems. Once all of the solutions are stated, it will be easier for our prospects to choose one solution.

When providing these solutions, we want to place the bad solutions first. The best solution, our solution, should be last. Our solution should be the last thing that our prospects hear.

Let's do a simple example of how this would sound in real life.

Prospect: "I think your multi-ingredient supplement is too expensive."

Us: "Yes, it is expensive. But let's look at the options. We could grow each ingredient in a small greenhouse that we build in our backyard. Of course this would take too much time, and in the end, would be much more expensive.

"A more practical solution would be to buy each ingredient individually at your local health food store. But if you added up the total spent on each raw ingredient, it would be far more than the price of our product.

"Our last option would be to purchase our product. We buy in bulk, put all the ingredients together so it is convenient, and it will end up at the best price for you.

"We know you want the benefits of this product. Which of these options seems like a better choice for you?"

Our prospect is relieved. He feels like he has options. Now, he needs to pick the best option for him.

Let's do an example for our business opportunity.

Prospect: "I am not sure I should join this business. Yes, it looks good, but I don't know."

Us: "Well, joining our business is not the only option. Let's look at your choices. First, we can hope that your boss gives you a 50% raise in salary, so that you could start paying off your credit cards and bills. That is not likely to happen, at least not in the next few days.

"Second, we can hope to win the lottery. Just kidding. You and I both know that is not a viable option.

"Third, you can start your own traditional business. This would put you further in debt. You would have to pay for office space, startup costs, inventory, and you would take a huge risk. Going further into debt is not a good option when you are trying to get out of debt.

"Fourth, you could join our business tonight. Start now so that you can begin to earn the money you need to pay off your credit cards and bills.

"So yes, you have options. You don't have an option of not doing anything, as these credit cards and bills have to be paid. So which of these options seems like the best choice for you right now?"

We removed the vague "I hope another option shows up" conversation in our prospects' minds. Now, the choices are clear. Our prospects have to make a choice. What will this choice be? Well, that is for our prospects to decide.

Why don't all of our prospects join?

Q. What do all of our presentations have in common?

A. They all offer time freedom and money freedom.

We will never have a prospect tell us:

"Oh, I don't want to join because I don't want any of that time freedom or money freedom. I would like more debt, less money, and more time at work."

Sounds silly, doesn't it?

If our prospects want time freedom and money freedom, and our presentation offers time freedom and money freedom, then why don't all our prospects join?

Because they aren't confident that they will achieve time freedom and money freedom with our opportunity. Sure, **we** can do it, but they don't think **they** can do it.

Now here is the key.

When prospects don't have confidence, here is what most presenters do:

They start introducing new benefits.

They tell the prospect about three-way calls, nice brochures, perfect videos, fancy meetings, car bonuses, and other benefits. But they are missing the point.

The prospect doesn't think he can do it, so it doesn't matter how good the benefits are.

The solution?

Instead of talking about more benefits, we should concentrate on showing our prospect how **simple** it can be to do our business. This would be a great time for our "one-minute presentation."

We must focus on our prospect's confidence in his chances of success in our business. That is what is holding our prospect back - confidence.

Reduce our objections.

Ever run across a steady stream of objections such as these?

"The marketing plan is too complicated."

"The products are too expensive."

"I don't know anybody."

"I could never learn all that nutrition talk."

"My friends are different."

"There is too much competition."

"I tried that but it never worked."

Sound familiar? Why do we get these objections?

Imagine we get a stream of objections about the start-up costs of our business opportunity.

Here is the big question. Are our program's start-up costs the real reason we get these objections?

No.

If the start-up costs caused these objections, then every distributor in our program would get the same objection at every presentation.

Look around. What do we see? We notice several leaders doing quite well with our program, and they don't have the start-up cost objection. Hmmm. Maybe the cause of this objection is not our program.

Okay. Let's look at our prospects. Maybe we are talking with prospects who won't spend money. Time to think again. All prospects spend money. All prospects buy. Our prospects are spending money with someone else instead of us. They have expensive cars and smartphones. When we leave a prospect's home, our prospect doesn't say, "I will never spend again."

Of course, our prospect will spend money again. The problem is that our prospect is not spending with us!

So, this objection is not from the company's start-up cost, and it is not coming from a prospect who doesn't spend money.

Then where else can we look?

We can look at ... ourselves.

Yes, we were at every presentation where this objection happened. We were at the "scene of the crime" every time.

So, what are we doing that causes objections?

Here is a little trick to discover what causes many of our objections.

Record our presentation. Then, in the quiet of our home, we can review our presentation.

When our prospect makes an objection, simply back up a minute or two in our recording. Check to see what we said that caused that objection.

We caused the objection? Yes. In most cases we triggered the objection with our choice of words.

With a little practice, and a little bit of humility, we can listen to our recording and hear the words and phrases we used that caused our prospect to react with an objection.

Are we saying that prospects are reactive?

Yes. Prospects are very reactive. They don't randomly come up with objections.

For example, let's say that we get the "pyramid objection" often. This objection comes from something we said or did. Think about it. We don't see prospects walking on the street and randomly throwing up their arms and yelling, "It is a pyramid!"

The only reason the pyramid objection occurred is because of something we said or did!

Try this with team members also.

When we ask our distributors to record their presentations, they may say, "Oh, I don't like listening to myself give a presentation."

We will have to think, "Then maybe your prospects don't like listening to your presentation either."

Try it. Record one or two presentations, and listen closely. As professionals, we will notice many things that we say or do that can be improved.

And finally, a very dangerous word.

We must be careful about using the word "why" when questioning our prospects.

Why?

Because our prospects have bad feelings and programs about the word "why" from childhood. When we were children and we did something wrong, our parents would ask us, "Why did you do that?" This made us feel guilty and embarrassed.

If we use the word "why" when questioning our prospects, it may build resistance to an open discussion. Our prospects might feel defensive and want to justify their positions.

What could we say instead?

The words "what" or "how" are good substitutes for the word "why" when we ask our prospects a question. Here are some examples of using the words "what" or "how" to rephrase our questions.

A. "Why are you hesitating?"

B. "What is the main concern you have that is causing you to hesitate?"

A. "Why don't you want to join?"

B. "What would happen if you joined now?"

A. "Why are you unsure?"

B. "How can I make it safe for you to get started right now?"

A. "Why don't you want to get started now?"

B. "How can I help you get started now?"

This one little change, avoiding the "why" word, might be the difference between our prospect moving forward, or rejecting our opportunity.

"Help me understand ..."

"What" and "how" are not the only words that we can substitute for the "why" word. With a little imagination, we will find the phrases and words that feel most comfortable for us.

Here is another phrase that we could use: "Help me understand ..."

Let's do a few examples.

- "Help me understand your concerns about moving forward."

- "Help me understand the reasons for putting off the extra income until later."

- "Please help me understand the parts of our business that you feel might be risky."

Remember, prospects react to the words and phrases we say. When our prospects give a "no" answer to our offer, we should always ask ourselves, "What did we say immediately before that answer that caused this reaction?"

Conclusion.

Closing is simply getting our prospects to move forward and take action. We help our prospects overcome their fear of change. Now they can improve their lives with our products and opportunity.

One close won't fit every situation, since our prospects are not identical. They have many different challenges in their lives.

Of all the closes presented in this book, choose the closes that fit your style and needs. Enjoy the journey.

Good luck closing!

THANK YOU.

Thank you for purchasing and reading this book. I hope you found some ideas that will work for you.

Before you go, would it be okay if I asked a small favor? Would you take just one minute and leave a sentence or two reviewing this book online? Your review can help others choose what they will read next. It would be greatly appreciated by many fellow readers.

I travel the world 240+ days each year.
Let me know if you want me to stop in your
area and conduct a live Big Al training.

→ **BigAlSeminars.com** ←

FREE Big Al Training Audios

Magic Words for Prospecting

plus Free eBook and the Big Al Report!

→ **BigAlBooks.com/free** ←

MORE BIG AL BOOKS

BIGALBOOKS.COM

Pre-Closing for Network Marketing
"Yes" Decisions Before The Presentation

Instead of selling to customers with facts, features and benefits, let's talk to prospects in a way they like. We can now get that "yes" decision first, so the rest of our presentation will be easy.

The One-Minute Presentation
Explain Your Network Marketing Business Like A Pro

Learn to make your business grow with this efficient, focused business presentation technique.

Retail Sales for Network Marketers
How to Get New Customers for Your MLM Business

Learn how to position your retail sales so people are happy to buy. Don't know where to find customers for your products and services? Learn how to market to people who want what you offer.

Getting "Yes" Decisions
What insurance agents and financial advisors can say to clients

In the new world of instant decisions, we need to master the words and phrases to successfully move our potential clients to lifelong clients. Easy … when we can read their minds and service their needs immediately.

3 Easy Habits For Network Marketing
Automate Your MLM Success

Use these habits to create a powerful stream of activity in your network marketing business.

Motivation. Action. Results.
How Network Marketing Leaders Move Their Teams

Learn the motivational values and triggers our team members have, and learn to use them wisely. By balancing internal motivation and external motivation methods, we can be more effective motivators.

The Four Color Personalities for MLM
The Secret Language for Network Marketing

Learn the skill to quickly recognize the four personalities and how to use magic words to translate your message.

Ice Breakers!
How To Get Any Prospect To Beg You For A Presentation

Create unlimited Ice Breakers on-demand. Your distributors will no longer be afraid of prospecting, instead, they will love prospecting.

How To Get Instant Trust, Belief, Influence and Rapport!
13 Ways To Create Open Minds By Talking To The Subconscious Mind

Learn how the pros get instant rapport and cooperation with even the coldest prospects. The #1 skill every new distributor needs.

First Sentences for Network Marketing
How To Quickly Get Prospects On Your Side

Attract more prospects and give more presentations with great first sentences that work.

How to Follow Up With Your Network Marketing Prospects
Turn Not Now Into Right Now!

Use the techniques in this book to move your prospects forward from "Not Now" to "Right Now!"

How To Prospect, Sell And Build Your Network Marketing Business With Stories

If you want to communicate effectively, add your stories to deliver your message.

26 Instant Marketing Ideas To Build Your Network Marketing Business

176 pages of amazing marketing lessons and case studies to get more prospects for your business immediately.

How To Build Network Marketing Leaders
Volume One: Step-By-Step Creation Of MLM Professionals

This book will give you the step-by-step activities to actually create leaders.

How To Build Network Marketing Leaders
Volume Two: Activities And Lessons For MLM Leaders

You will find many ways to change people's viewpoints, to change their beliefs, and to reprogram their actions.

51 Ways and Places to Sponsor New Distributors
Discover Hot Prospects For Your Network Marketing Business

Learn the best places to find motivated people to build your team and your customer base.

Big Al's MLM Sponsoring Magic

How To Build A Network Marketing Team Quickly

This book shows the beginner exactly what to do, exactly what to say, and does it through the eyes of a brand-new distributor.

Public Speaking Magic

Success and Confidence in the First 20 Seconds

By using any of the three major openings in this book, we can confidently start our speeches and presentations without fear.

Worthless Sponsor Jokes

Network Marketing Humor

Here is a collection of worthless sponsor jokes from 25 years of the "Big Al Report." Network marketing can be enjoyable, and we can have fun making jokes along the way.

Start SuperNetworking!

5 Simple Steps to Creating Your Own Personal Networking Group

Start your own personal networking group and have new, pre-sold customers and prospects come to you.

How To Get Kids To Say Yes!

Using the Secret Four Color Languages to Get Kids to Listen

Turn discipline and frustration into instant cooperation. Kids love to say "yes" when they hear their own color-coded language.

BigAlBooks.com

ABOUT THE AUTHORS

Keith Schreiter has 20+ years of experience in network marketing and MLM. He shows network marketers how to use simple systems to build a stable and growing business.

So, do you need more prospects? Do you need your prospects to commit instead of stalling? Want to know how to engage and keep your group active? If these are the types of skills you would like to master, you will enjoy his "how-to" style.

Keith speaks and trains in the U.S., Canada, and Europe.

Tom "Big Al" Schreiter has 40+ years of experience in network marketing and MLM. As the author of the original "Big Al" training books in the late '70s, he has continued to speak in over 80 countries on using the exact words and phrases to get prospects to open up their minds and say "YES."

His passion is marketing ideas, marketing campaigns, and how to speak to the subconscious mind in simplified, practical ways. He is always looking for case studies of incredible marketing campaigns that give usable lessons.

As the author of numerous audio trainings, Tom is a favorite speaker at company conventions and regional events.

Lightning Source UK Ltd.
Milton Keynes UK
UKHW02f2329051217
313922UK00001B/3/P